PUSHING YOURSELF to POWER

JOHN e. PETERSON

Strength & Honor

BRONZE BOW PUB

PUSHING YOURSELF *to* POWER

All Scripture quotations, unless otherwise indicated, are taken from the Holy Bible, New International Version®. NIV®. Copyright © 1973, 1978, 1984 by International Bible Society. Used by permission of Zondervan Publishing House. All rights reserved.

ISBN 1-932458-01-8

Published by Bronze Bow Publishing Inc.,
2600 E. 26th Street, Minneapolis, MN 55406.

You can reach us on the Internet at www.bronzebowpublishing.com

Literary development and cover/interior design by
Koechel Peterson & Associates, Inc., Minneapolis, Minnesota.

Manufactured in the United States of America

Printed by Diversified Graphics Incorporated, Minneapolis, MN

TABLE OF CONTENTS

ACKNOWLEDGMENTS

One of the greatest lessons anyone can learn in life is that we succeed or fail oftentimes as a direct result of those we have chosen as friends, mentors, confidants, and business associates. In writing this acknowledgment, I wish to thank those who have been a guiding light and sustaining influence upon me and the development of this book.

These friends include:

The woman of my dreams, for your constant encouragement and belief in me and this project. Thanks for being mine!

David Koechel, my lifelong friend and business partner, for your continual support, encouragement, and unwavering commitment to excellence in all that you do.

Lance Wubbels, publisher of Bronze Bow Publishing, whose literary gifts and talents are without equal. Thank you, Lance, for using them on my behalf.

Tom Henry, whose artistry with a camera has been verified yet another time. Hey, Tom, it speaks volumes about your ability when you can make even me look pretty good.

Gregory Rohm, whose design excellence and ceaseless devotion to this project are evident on every page. Thank you, Gregory. I owe you one.

Duff Smith, the rock who makes sure it all happens when it is supposed to happen.

Matt Furey, whose friendship, guidance, and encouragement have made this book possible. Matt, believe me, I know that if it weren't for you and all I've learned because of you, this book would never have been written. Thank you, my friend.

Jim and Valerie Saxion, for your friendship, trust, and continued loyalty and always setting an example of what it means to be real and authentic.

Within a period of months you can create your own unique exercise machine. It will be better than any device you could possibly buy, has a lifetime guarantee, and, best of all, *will cost you nothing*. It will allow you to exercise your body with infinite combinations of variable force and speed, from variable angles and positions, and with variable ranges of motion. This machine will be capable of challenging the absolute limits of your strength, speed, endurance, flexibility, balance, coordination, and aesthetics, thus enhancing all seven vital attributes of true athletic fitness.

It will have a built-in computer complete with its own cooling system that instantly senses your body's changes in heat and energy production, and adjusts its force and speed to keep you from injuring yourself. It will sense any sore spots in your body, or potential points of injury, and will instantly adjust its force and tempo to automatically compensate so you don't accidentally aggravate that condition. This machine is so portable you can take it with you wherever you go, and so compact you can give yourself a complete workout in a very limited amount of space. You have always owned the parts to this machine.

This machine is your own body!

And this is your instruction manual. By using John Peterson's *Transformetrics*™ *Training System* to train your body, you will create the ultimate exercise machine.

This Book Is for You

Pushing Yourself to Power is for every man, woman, boy, or girl who truly wants to achieve a strong, healthy, beautifully shaped body that exudes energy, vitality, and a joy for living. It's for all the busy people who simply don't have the time to go to a gym, and particularly for moms and dads who are already overwhelmed with other obligations. It's for athletes of all types who want to dramatically increase their all-around functional fitness and strength. And it's for everyone who wants to follow the road to dynamic strength and vibrant good health.

Here are some of the many benefits you will experience as a direct result of the study and application of *Transformetrics*™ *Training System.*

1. **A bulging waistline will disappear** and be replaced by beautifully toned abdominal muscles.

2. **Both your lower and upper back will be dramatically strengthened and made more flexible.** For many people, all forms of back pain will be completely eliminated.

3. **Functional strength, flexibility, endurance, balance, speed, and coordination will be enhanced** so much that it will be difficult to put a percentage on it. But let's just say 500 percent for starters.

4. **You will handle daily stress far better,** which will improve your circulation, digestion, and thought processes.

5. **You will sleep soundly** and awake feeling refreshed, recharged, and revitalized.

6. **You will have a much calmer demeanor** as you develop nerves of steel and a mind that has a laser-like focus.

7. **You will master the ultimate exercise system that requires no gym or expensive equipment,** and that you can follow as easily at home as on the road.

INTRODUCTION

"Present suffering is not enjoyable, but life would be worth little without it. The difference between iron and steel is fire, but steel is worth all its cost."

—Maltbie Babcock

Meeting Mac Anderson

Early in the summer of 2002, I had the pleasure of meeting the famed motivational speaker and Founder of Successories®, Mac Anderson. He had just signed a book contract with a close friend of mine, Jack Countryman, the "J" of J. Countryman Publishers. Jack wanted our company, Koechel Peterson & Associates, Inc., to handle the design and packaging of Mac's book, *The Nature of Success*. So when Mac wanted to meet the team that would be handling the design, Jack arranged for us to meet.

From the moment we met, it was clear to me, to my business partner, Dave Koechel, and to Lance Wubbels, our Vice President of Literary Development, that Mac was cut from the same cloth as Jack Countryman. Everything this man did had to be done to the highest standard of excellence. It was obvious that Mac had not become Mac Anderson by leaving anything to chance.

After a morning meeting where we discussed every issue that concerned Mac about his book, we headed out for lunch. Stepping into the midday heat, I took off my sport coat, preferring the black stretch T-shirt I had underneath. As we were getting into the car, Mac said, "Well, John, how many hours a day do you spend at the gym to look like that?" I took this as a genuine compliment, coming from a man who obviously put forth the time and effort to always stay in great shape.

I first thanked Mac for the compliment, then added, "I don't train at a gym, Mac. I train at home with

my own system of exercise that's based on the Charles Atlas training program. I've been doing it since I was about ten years old . . . after having recovered from polio."

"Really? So you don't lift weights?"

"No. Just my body weight."

"How much time do you spend at it each day?" Mac asked.

"Oh, forty-five minutes to an hour at most."

"Wow! That's incredible," he said. "You should write a book on it."

"Wait Till You Hit Forty"

Over the years, friends and students whom I've trained in the martial arts and physical conditioning have often asked me to write a book that explained the exact methods, techniques, and philosophy of health that I have used to attain my strength and fitness. But this request from Mac Anderson carried considerable weight. In fact, his comments finally motivated me to write this book.

Actually, every time I take my wife on a scuba diving trip to the Caribbean, whether it's to Jamaica or the Florida Keys, someone is always asking how I built my physique, how I stay in shape, or if I'm a personal trainer.

True story. In January 2002, my wife, Denise, and I had just come in from a five-mile swim at the Grand Lido Resort in Negril, Jamaica. A guest at the resort approached us, started talking about personal fitness, and asked me why he never saw me at the gym. After I told him how I trained, he grunted and said, "Wait till you hit forty. It won't be so easy to keep your stomach muscles looking that tight." At that point, Denise broke into laughter and said, "You made my Johnny's day! He's turning fifty this year." The man looked incredulous and immediately asked me, "What's your birth date?" So I told him it was October 25, 1952. "Un-____ believable" was all he said as he walked away.

I say this not to boast, but to simply relate that the exercise program my grandfather and "Uncle Wally" started me on at the age of ten is superb. It was a hybrid taken from programs developed by two of the world's most famous bodybuilders of the 1920s, Earle E. Liederman and Charles Atlas. It's a program that has been verified by two of my close friends, who also teach systems based entirely on body-weight strength and conditioning exercises. One friend is ex-Navy SEAL, Mark De Lisle, whose *Navy SEAL Breakthrough to Master Level Fitness* book is a must read. The other is Matt Furey, whose world famous *Combat Conditioning* system has sparked a revolution in strength and conditioning, especially among grapplers. Both men offer incredible methods for physical transformation and conditioning.

How I Got Started

Born in October 1952, I was the third child and second son in my family, and another sister and brother followed me. Our family was typical of other post-World War II families. My dad and uncles were battle-hardened war veterans who had seen and experienced what no one should ever see or experience. Having lived through the Great Depression and fought to save humanity from insane dictators, all these men wanted was a chance to come home, get married, work hard, and raise a family. They were real MEN!

These men tried hard to do everything right. They taught us a profound respect for country and a faith in God. Both my dad and mom were deeply religious and raised us in a fundamentalist church.

But even so, my dad was always willing to make exceptions about going to movies (a no-no in our church) as long as John Wayne was the star.

I was healthy until Thanksgiving 1956, when I contracted polio. My folks spent a great deal of time and money getting me well, but once the doctors determined I was in the clear, there was still one problem. The poliovirus had left my legs dreadfully misshapen. In order to straighten them, both legs had to be broken in several places, reset, and placed in casts from my feet to my upper thighs. Due to the nerve damage of polio, this had to be done *without* any anesthetic. My mother still says that it was one of the worst days of her life when she held me as they broke my legs. She said she was certain I'd grow up to be a boxer, because after the doctors made the initial break, I hit one of them with an incredibly hard punch before I passed out.

Part of my recovery involved the use of crutches, which I kind of liked because my forearms got so developed using them that my little friends started calling me "Popeye." My older sister, Diane, used to draw anchor tattoos on my forearms just like Popeye's. About the only drawback to the crutches came in the form of the neighborhood bully, who was two years older and the ultimate jerk. He loved to pick on little kids, and in my case that meant kicking my crutches out from under me. He was so mean he beat his dog with a baseball bat and threw rotten eggs at old people's houses for kicks.

I have this clown, in part, to thank for starting me on a quest to become strong, fit, and able to defend myself. It came in one of those moments that transform your life, though at the time it seems as though it's anything but that. It happened during the summer when I was ten years old.

I was at the park with some of my friends when the neighborhood bully showed up and started slapping around my friend Jeffy and making fun of his glasses. I told the creep to "leave him alone. You're a lot bigger than he is."

The big bad bully turned his focus toward me and said, "What's the little cripple gonna do about it?"

I should have kept my mouth shut, but instead I said something along the lines of, "Why don't you fat slobs ever pick on somebody your own size?"

That did it. He was enraged and came crashing down on me before I could run. Picture me at a scrawny 94 pounds pinned beneath a nearly thirteen-year-old kid, who's over six feet tall and over 300 pounds of blubber, and who's telling me he's going to pound me within an inch of my life.

"Leave me alone or my brother Al will pound you!" I cried out, hoping a threat might prevail. Al was twelve and going through adolescence. He was very strong for his age and a natural athlete. He could throw faster than any other kid in the entire baseball league, even faster than our coaches.

The bully just laughed and said, "Your brother ain't here, cripple, and even if he was, I'd just beat him up first."

He started to pound on me, but suddenly I heard Al yell at him from about ten feet away. "Get off my brother, you fat slob."

Before Goliath rolled off me, he slapped me upside the head as hard as he could. "I'm gonna finish what I started just as soon as I beat your brother."

Slowly he got up and turned around to charge my brother. What he didn't expect was that Al was in his pitcher's stance, waiting with a baseball in his right hand for his target to be exposed.

Of all the pitches I'd ever seen my brother throw, none compared to the speed and accuracy of that pitch. If my brother was expecting a "no hitter," he got it! The guy hit the ground like a gutted rhino, writhing in agony and foaming at the mouth.

Okay, so now you're wondering where my brother nailed the bully. I'll tell you, but I must be discreet because my mom will read these words. As stated previously, she and my dad were committed fundamentalist Christians, and they taught me to believe in God's miraculous power. Based on that belief, I'll just say that if that guy was ever able to father children after getting nailed by my brother's fastest fastball, believe me, *it's a miracle!*

Grandpa and Uncle Wally

I arrived home badly shaken by the experience, my swollen face hurt, but I was glad to have all my teeth. Fortunately, I was able to spend the weekend at my grandfather's house. Grandpa was no ordinary man. He was a long-time physical culturist, had a great physique, exercised every day, and had followed the Charles Atlas system since he read about it in McFadden's *Physical Culture* magazine in November 1921. Grandpa also had a close friend whom we called "Uncle Wally," who had followed Earle Liederman's course in the mid 1920s when he was a young Marine. Both men were perfect physical specimens. To this day, Uncle Wally is the only guy I've ever seen who could chin himself 6 times with either arm. (He warned me, though, that if I tried it too often it causes "the mother of all tendinitis.")

When I told Grandpa and Uncle Wally about what happened, they tried to not laugh, but it was hard for them. When I finished, my grandfather ruffled my hair with his right hand and said, "Well, Jackson, we've got work to do. If your mouth is going to get you in trouble, you better learn how to back it up."

Grandpa pulled out an original copy of the Charles Atlas course from the early 1920s. As we went through it, Uncle Wally added information from the Liederman course that he had committed to memory in 1925. With all that information in hand, I was ready to start, except for one thing. In all sincerity, I asked Grandpa and Uncle Wally if it was really okay for me to begin.

"Sure it is, Jackson," my grandpa replied. "Why do you ask?"

"Well," I replied, "because Atlas was a 97-pound weakling when he started, and I only weigh 94 pounds."

After the two men stopped laughing, they reassured me that it was okay.

I took to the Atlas exercises with a vengeance. I didn't have any muscles, so I just practiced smiling like Atlas did in those famous ads where the scrawny guy gets sand kicked in his face and comes back later to knock the bully on his butt once and for all. But what I lacked in muscle I made up for in determination, and it wasn't long before I was packing on some serious muscle. By the time I was twelve, I was the only kid at our

school who could walk the entire perimeter of the gym floor on his hands. And I was also the only kid who could perform 16 pull-ups. When I was nearly fifteen, I was almost my full adult height of 5'10-1/2", weighed 165 pounds of solid muscle (just 17 pounds lighter than my present weight), and could do 39 pull-ups. I was the strongest and fittest kid in my class, doing 500 push-ups a day in sets of 100 as well as the full range of Atlas exercises.

From there I took up an intense interest in the martial arts and worked hard to earn black belts and proficiency in several of them over the years. Currently, I'm studying the Russian martial art called "Systema," and it's the best I've encountered in my fifty years on this planet.

So now that you know about me, it's time for us to focus on you. Let's get going! (Oh, by the way, I am the guy you see in over 90 percent of the pictures in this book. If you don't like the look or type of physique, better to stop now and try something else.)

"There is a principle which is a bar against all information, which is proof against all argument, and which cannot fail to keep a man in everlasting ignorance. That principle is condemnation before investigation."

— Noel Johnson
author of *A Dud at 70, A Stud at 80*

STARTING OUT RIGHT

Your Current Physical Condition

Before beginning *any* exercise program, you should always consult with a physician—period. And under no conditions should you begin my program unless you can honestly answer no to all of the following questions.

1) Has your doctor ever said that you have a heart condition, and that you should only do physical activity that is performed under a doctor's supervision?

2) Do you ever feel pain in your chest when you do physical activity?

3) In the past three months, have you had chest pain when you were doing physical work, such as shoveling snow or raking leaves?

4) Do you lose your balance due to dizziness, or do you ever lose consciousness?

5) Do you currently have a problem with bone, joint, tendon, ligament, or muscle tears that could be made worse by a change in your daily physical activity?

6) Is your doctor prescribing you medication of any kind for a blood pressure, circulatory, or heart condition?

7) Do you know of any other reason why you should not engage in a physical exercise program or activity?

Exercise Duration

In general, you need to devote at least 30 minutes every day to the exercises contained in this book. However, it is not necessary to do all 30 minutes at one time. Many people whom I have trained could not do 10 consecutive Furey Push-ups, 20 Furey Squats, or even touch their toes when they started, yet you wouldn't believe what they can do now. So don't worry that you aren't strong, athletic, and fit

right now. If you were, you wouldn't need me or this book.

Bottom line: Regardless of your present physical condition, I'm glad you're here.

The Most Important Exercises

I call them the *Dynamic Three*. They are the Furey Push-up, the Furey Squat, and the Atlas Push-up. And if you are either a grappler or combat sports aficionado, I add one other exercise to my list—the Furey Bridge.

The Furey Push-up

If you can't do these three or four exercises at first, don't let it concern you. I'll give you a complete program that will have you doing these exercises in no time. The important thing is to make a commitment to yourself and your well-being and to stick with it on a daily basis. *If* you do, you *will* be thrilled. Your form will improve as your strength, flexibility, stamina, and balance improve simultaneously. I know all about it. At the beginning, my form wasn't great, and after all these years I'm still striving for flawless form on every repetition.

Remember: If you put off starting until you can do it perfectly, you'll never begin. So let's put pride and ego aside and get started now.

Minimums and Maximums

The suggestions I give you for starting repetitions are simply that—*suggestions*. As you come to understand the **Transformetrics**™ *Training System* and learn exactly how the Dynamic Visualized Resistance (**DVR**) and Dynamic Self-Resistance (**DSR**) exercises are performed, you will notice two incredible changes happening simultaneously. Your strength will skyrocket, and your ability to maintain a laser-like focus of mind over muscle will give you a complete sense of body awareness and self-mastery you may never have experienced until now.

For this reason, you will do *fewer* repetitions of each exercise and *fewer* sets (number of times you repeat an exercise). This is due to the fact that your intensity (the amount of force or contraction applied to each exercise) is so much greater. This is contrary to what many other so-called experts have students do, but think about it. As you become much stronger and apply much greater intensity (force), you need *fewer* reps, *not more*. Otherwise you will exhaust yourself.

Transformetrics™ **is about training smarter, not longer.** It's like Uncle Wally used to say to me: "You can train one of two ways. You can train long or you can train hard—but you can't do both!"

As far as maximums are concerned, there was a time when I was curious about how many reps are really maximum. So I sent a letter with my pictures and measurements to Charles Roman, who had been Charles Atlas's business partner, to show what I had achieved with the "Charles Atlas Dynamic Tension Training System." In that letter I asked specifically about how many repetitions Mr. Atlas had done for each exercise. I received back a letter from Charles Roman that gave me the exact numbers of repetitions Mr. Atlas performed on a daily basis during his prime years.

(And yes, I still have the letter if anyone wants to challenge me.)

I was surprised to discover that for some of the exercises I was performing more reps than Charles Atlas. So, in terms of maximums, it's really up to the individual. You'll see how true this is when you read the Success Profiles in this book.

Bottom line: There is no preset limit to what the human body can do *provided the mind is in agreement*.

Sculpted and Ripped Muscles

Yes! The *Transformetrics*™ *Training System* will give you sculpted and ripped muscles if it is complemented by the "Ripped to the Bone" diet recommendations at the back of this book. But this powerful combination will do far, far more than just make you look great. In addition to being stronger, leaner, and more muscular, you will experience a dramatic increase in functional fitness. That means you'll increase your strength, flexibility, speed, stamina, balance, and coordination. This is the kind of fitness you expect to find only in gymnasts, rock climbers, grapplers, and martial artists.

By contrast, bodybuilders do not have functional muscles. Their muscles are stiff, tight, and cramped in situations that require agility. John Madden, the legendary football coach and television commentator, noted that some of the most frequently and severely injured players seemed to be those who had massively developed muscles from heavy weight training. In addition, most bodybuilders don't have a great deal of endurance. And despite their huge mass, most of them are not very functionally strong.

If you want excessive muscle mass, study bodybuilding. If you want a beautifully proportioned, lithe, hard, ultra-strong, and functionally fit body, you've got the guidebook in your hands right now in *Pushing Yourself to Power*.

Clothing and Equipment

Most of you who follow my program will be doing it in the privacy of your home. If such is the case, you'll be most comfortable in minimal clothing. Charles Atlas recommended that his students train in the nude as the ancient Grecian athletes did, but that's your call.

If you can, I recommend that you exercise in front of a large mirror so you can observe your form and the workings of your musculature. Other than that, you really don't need anything but a towel and a soft surface for the Bridging exercises. As far as what to wear on your feet, I recommend training barefoot whenever possible, which helps to strengthen the feet.

Rhythm

I've been asked if I will release exercise videos that incorporate full workouts. Although I have no problem with doing a video series that carefully details every exercise technique, I'm hesitant to do workout videos. It is just too easy for viewers to think it's important to keep up with me. I believe it is vitally important for every person to train at his or her *own* pace and tempo, and not at someone else's. I would much prefer that you focus on flawless technique and not worry about how or at what speed someone else is doing it.

Here's the point: Do the exercises at the pace and rhythm that is exactly right for you. Don't try to imitate someone else's style or rhythm, because if you do, you'll always feel second-rate and dependent on someone else. I don't want you to ever feel that way. After all, this book is about freedom from all that.

Focused Breathing

As you start training, you'll notice your breathing takes on a deep natural rhythm all its own. You won't need to consciously try to breathe in a certain fashion. This is because the exercises in this program literally cause you to naturally breathe deeply. So don't worry about how to breathe—just breathe and stay focused on the objective of the beautifully developed physique you are acquiring. You will gain far greater results this way than if you allow your mind to worry about how you are breathing.

Remember: Everything I'm teaching you is about going from feeling you've gone *nowhere* in your physical training to a point of satisfaction where you can say, "Thank God, I'm *Now Here*."

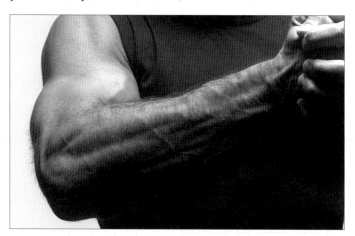

More Than Just Physical Changes

The *Transformetrics™ Training System* will develop every muscle in your body evenly and naturally from your neck to your toes. The strength ratios in your various muscle groups will change dramatically as will your flexibility, stamina, balance, speed, and agility.

Yes, you're in for a wonderful time of self-discovery, which in turn leads to major psychological benefits. The other obvious benefit will be that your internal organs will improve their functions. In fact, sometimes the changes are quite dramatic. This is especially evident in your energy levels and libido (which depending upon your viewpoint can be a blessing or a curse).

Weight Loss and Reduced Body Fat

These exercises when combined with a good wholesome diet such as the one outlined in Lesson Two on Nutrition will go a long way toward speeding up your metabolism and helping you shred body fat. Unquestionably, the best results are obtained by the right combination of diet and exercise taken together. But even if you don't want to follow this diet plan, a general rule to follow is simply to avoid white starchy foods that come in bags, boxes, or wrappers.

How Long Do You Need to Follow This Program?

How long do you plan to live? How long do you plan to brush your teeth or take a shower? How long do you want to be able to walk or run or enjoy a rewarding intimate relationship with your spouse?

I can't answer those questions for you. But the answer for me is simple. *Life is movement.* Once you stop moving, it won't be long before you can't move. And once that happens, you're dead.

So I encourage you to choose life every moment of every single day that God has given you.

How Do You Know That This Program Is Everything That I Say It Is?

I ask you to read this book with an open mind and heart, and then memorize the following quote and apply its message to every part of your life. If you do, the answer to the above questions will be self-evident.

"Do not believe in anything simply because you have heard it. Do not believe in anything simply because it is spoken and rumored by many. Do not believe in anything simply because it is found written in your religious books. Do not believe in anything merely on the authority of teachers and elders. Do not believe in traditions because they have been handed down for many generations. But after observation and analysis, when you find that anything agrees with reason and is conducive to the good and benefit of one and all, then accept it and live up to it."

THE 7 ATTRIBUTES OF DYNAMIC FUNCTIONAL FITNESS

Fitness experts often refer to *functional fitness*, but virtually none of them define what it means to be *functionally fit*. I hear them state that "functional fitness is fitness you can use in sport and everyday life," but how vague is that? Generalities don't cut it when it comes to fitness or how it applies to you in everyday life or athletics. Which is why I want you to have a complete understanding of what *true* functional fitness is, and why the *Transformetrics*™ *Training System* is second to none in helping you develop it.

When I use the term functional fitness, I'm referring to seven distinct and separate physical attributes that can and should be developed simultaneously. The attributes are as follows:

1. **Strength**
2. **Flexibility**
3. **Endurance**
4. **Speed**
5. **Balance**
6. **Coordination**
7. **Aesthetics**

Though I have listed the attributes in a certain order, the truth is that none is more important than another. They are equally important.

1. Strength

When you move large pieces of furniture, take a big dog for a walk in the park, or open a stubborn jar of pickles, you need *strength*. A person who appears to be muscular may actually be quite weak in terms of *functional strength*. A slender, meek person may be far stronger than a large, menacing-looking person.

True strength depends upon the quality of your muscles, and it may be hereditary or acquired through training. Strength is a factor that should not be emphasized at the expense of all other fitness attributes. If it is, a person can become quite stiff and unable to use their strength. While watching a video from a man who claimed to have the ultimate program to a warrior's strength and fitness, I noted that he was demonstrating overhead presses while sitting on a bench with his back supported. This man is very muscular, but the contours of his muscles are not pleasing to the eye, and he had obvious difficulty doing just a few repetitions with a 90-pound barbell. His muscles were so tight that it literally made him *muscle bound* and not able to use his strength. The same thing can happen to women who spend their time doing only weight training exercises.

A woman should be able to carry a bag of groceries in one arm and a baby in the other without dropping either. A man should be able to lift his own weight with ease, climb a rope using only his hands, and carry heavy luggage or another person from a burning building.

Strength wisely developed as a part of a total fitness program will serve you well. And you must exercise daily to maintain it. When you work on your strength factor, your body is firm, your muscles beautifully toned, and your physique or figure is at your best. So while strength should not be over-emphasized at the expense of every other attribute, it is nonetheless crucially important and must not be de-emphasized either.

2. Flexibility

Tying your shoes, getting into a car, picking flowers, bowling, playing with children, or swinging a tennis racket or golf club requires flexibility. Even the simplest activities require some bending, reaching, or twisting. Therefore, you need suppleness in the joints of your body and flexibility in your muscle tissue.

By following the *Transformetrics™ Training System* that simultaneously develops strength, flexibility, balance, coordination, speed, and endurance, anyone can increase the suppleness of their joints and the flexibility of their muscles. And the opposite is just as true. If a person trains in a wrong way, he may become unmanageably stiff due to the overdevelopment of one part of the body and the underdevelopment of another. Meanwhile, a weak, slim, or even a plump person who is physically untrained can be so flexible and supple as to be almost collapsible.

Keep in mind that many factors affect a person's flexibility. Some of the factors include the length of limbs in relation to torso, the state of tension or relaxation, and even the ambient temperature of any given setting.

And though flexibility is vitally important in preventing muscle and joint injury, the acquisition of flexibility must be kept in line with the other attributes of true fitness. I have a friend who is a yoga instructor and as flexible as a rag doll, but he can't do a single pull-up. If he were ever accosted by a thug on the street, he'd be unable to defend himself. But who knows, maybe he could just bend out of the way.

3. Endurance

When taking a long walk between terminals at an airport, climbing two or three flights of stairs, performing errands, mowing the lawn, or doing a simple chore such as washing the windows brings on any sign of fatigue, you are revealing a lack of endurance.

Endurance is the factor that helps your energy last over a long period of time, and you call upon it constantly. Long distance runners and swimmers and all durable performers, such as those you see at Cirque du Soliel or a ballet company, are able to perfect their endurance by undergoing specialized training. By improving your lung capacity and breathing patterns as well as strengthening your heart muscles, you can train yourself to resist fatigue and make anything you do easier, from driving a golf ball great distances to playing 18 holes without fatigue.

4. Speed

Okay, I'll be honest with you. I only know one man who is as fast as a speeding bullet, and that man is my good friend Clark Kent. But what I am referring to here is not about speeding bullets. It's about practicality. So let's look at speed.

Whether it's a work deadline, a close tennis match, or a bus to be caught, you need speed to perform rapid body movements. This attribute helps you do anything quickly and to the best of your ability when under pressure. The faster your muscles obey the nerve impulses they receive, the faster you can physically perform and respond.

Speed may refer to an isolated action of a part of your body, such as the legs or forearms, or to the combined action of multiple areas of the body, such as is required in sprinting on the football field or racing in a swimming pool. If you can get into a fast revolving door easily, catch a fastball,

grasp a tow rope on the ski slope, or jump into a New York City taxi cab before it takes off, you have adequate speed.

Besides being a lifesaver in critical moments when you need to dodge a reckless driver or avoid a falling object, speed is useful in countless daily tasks and in all active sports. However, speed is one factor that requires careful control or you will "overstrain your brakes" or swing too quickly and miss your aim. Your speed needs adjusting in any sport as well as each time you rush during a pressured day.

There are two types of speed: *initial speed*, which helps you initiate a fast action or response; and *maximum speed*, which is the highest pace or fastest action that your body can produce.

Strong, well-conditioned muscles that have been developed in the proper way will help you move faster.

5. Balance

It's wonderful to know that your body is *strong, flexible*, and *enduring*. But if you stop and think about it, you would not be able to develop any of these three athletic attributes if you had no sense of balance.

Balance is crucial to every sport, whether it's golf, skiing, tennis, distance running, or Olympic weightlifting. And it is just as important in daily life. For instance, have you ever walked down an icy street in Chicago in the middle of a January snowstorm with wind gusts so strong you felt they could knock you down? If you have, you understand how important balance is. Climbing a ladder to change a light bulb or walking up a flight of stairs with a baby in your arms is dangerous if you don't have a good sense of balance. The truth is that no matter what you do, you will do it better if you can perfect your balance.

6. Coordination

The payoff for the perfection of the preceding attributes is coordination. We see exciting examples of human coordination on the ballet stage or watch any number of sports events. And we especially see it in ourselves when we execute simple or complex movements.

By means of coordination, we function harmoniously and precisely. Without it, strength, flexibility, endurance, speed, and balance are as useless as a Ferrari without a driver.

When you are well-coordinated, specific skills, such as skiing, mowing the lawn, or trimming the shrubs, seem far less taxing than before. Unlike the animal kingdom where coordination is far more instinctual, human beings must practice in order to maintain or increase the coordination of muscular skills. Likewise, humans lose their coordination if they don't stay in practice. A perfect example of this is found in what happens to a person who has been bedridden for some time and then tries to walk.

Here's the good news. Everyone can improve their coordination with the right exercise program that allows the body to move through multiple planes of movement. Remember that history has shown us time after time that with true dedication even an awkward youngster with weak arms and no stamina, and who gets sand kicked in his face, can transform himself into Charles Atlas.

7. Aesthetics

Aesthetics refers to how your body looks and how you feel about the way it looks. Although there are many reasons why people of all ages embark on strength, fitness, and weight-loss programs, there is none that even remotely compares to the motivation of aesthetics. This is because how you look is directly related to your self-image. This is also why magazine ads for bodybuilding courses have always focused on this one attribute. And tell me, have you ever seen an infomercial for exercise or weight-loss products on television that didn't focus on aesthetics?

The bottom line is simple. There has never been a man who didn't wish he could have a lithe, hard, muscular physique. And there has never been a woman who didn't wish she had a gorgeous sculpted figure. If this were not true, television infomercials selling exercise equipment would not be running practically around the clock. This also why cosmetic plastic surgery, stomach stapling, liposuction, breast implants for women, and pectoral implants for men have become so popular.

But this book isn't about quick fixes. It's about *complete, lifelong change* that will enhance every facet of your life. And, yes, that means aesthetically as well. It is not possible to develop high level fitness without it showing. If you want a beautiful physique or figure, abundant good health, and complete mastery over every facet of your life, that is within your control. You'll find the methods and strategies to accomplish it within the pages of this book.

Question & Answer

Q: At what point should a person begin the *Transformetrics™ Training System*?

A: It would be great if every person started taking their health seriously while still in their early twenties, but any time you connect with this message can be the right time to start. I've seen guys in their late thirties who already looked like the portrait of Dorian Gray *after* the painting got slashed. And I've also seen men such as my friend Jack Countryman who is in his mid-seventies and has the strength and stamina of a man thirty years younger. The choice is yours. But just as the Bible says, "Today is the day of salvation," so too is today the day of *rejuvenation*.

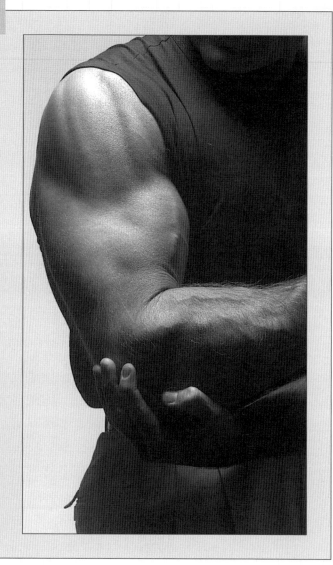

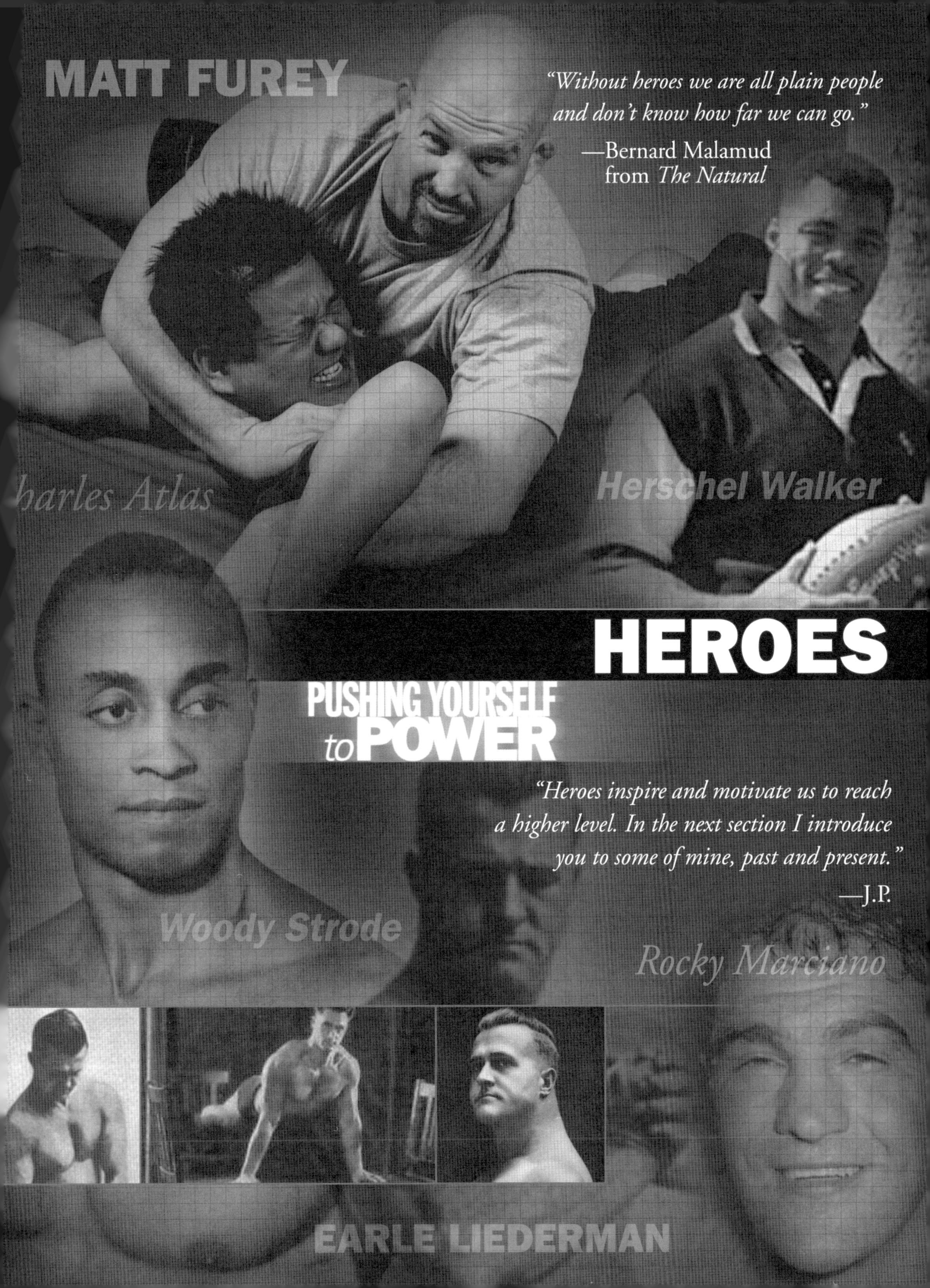

MATT FUREY
Charles Atlas
Herschel Walker
Woody Strode
Rocky Marciano
EARLE LIEDERMAN

"Without heroes we are all plain people and don't know how far we can go."
—Bernard Malamud
from *The Natural*

HEROES

PUSHING YOURSELF to POWER

"Heroes inspire and motivate us to reach a higher level. In the next section I introduce you to some of mine, past and present."
—J.P.

EARLE E. LIEDERMAN
THE FATHER OF MODERN BODYBUILDING

"Far better is it to dare mighty things, to win glorious triumphs, even though checkered by failure...than to rank with those poor spirits who neither enjoy much nor suffer much, because they live in a gray twilight that knows not victory nor defeat."

—THEODORE ROOSEVELT

After conducting a thorough and intensive research into the foundations of modern bodybuilding, I'm convinced that the man who was most instrumental in creating and elevating the American public's awareness of strength and physical conditioning was Earle E. Liederman. Throughout the late 1910s and all of the 1920s, Earle was the undisputed King of the Mail-Order Bodybuilders. Even to this day, several of his books are considered to be among the most thorough and well-conceived books ever published on the topic of strength and physical development.

The details of Earle's life are difficult to determine because he seldom discussed his private life. Even the date of his birth is uncertain. But it is believed that he was born in 1886 in Brooklyn, New York, to Swedish immigrant parents, and he graduated from high school in Jamaica, New York. After receiving his diploma, he pursued a degree in physical education and was hired by the New York Board of Education soon after graduation.

While working for the Board of Education, Earle also tried his hand at boxing. It didn't take him long, however, to realize that his greater talents were outside the boxing ring. He then tried wrestling, which also proved to not be his strong suit. But soon after his stint as a wrestler, he was convinced by a talent scout that with his superb physical development and obvious good looks he would do well as a strong man on the vaudeville circuit. The year was 1910, and Earle discovered his calling and destiny.

For more than eight years, Earle toured the circuit and was a huge success. It was during this time he met and started a partnership with a young man by the name of Charles Atlas. Together they toured the Orpheum Circuit, giving countless demonstrations of strength, gymnastic feats, and muscle control. They were incredibly popular and sold out theaters across the United States.

The Mail-Order Exercise Course

Earle Liederman's theatrical stint developed his showmanship and confidence, but eventually he tired of life on the road. In 1919 he decided to put into action a long cherished plan to publish his exercise regimen and sell it through the mail. Due to all the requests he had received over the years, he knew there was a waiting audience.

And Earle knew his course would work for anyone. After all, throughout his years of touring there were months that went by when he couldn't get to a gym (there were none). During those years, he created his own system of exercise that was primarily *free hand* resistance exercises, with a few exercises that required his favorite form of apparatus, an elastic chest expander. The entire course was written so that anyone could train at home and attain a superb development just as he had done.

To promote the course, Earle wrote a series of powerful ads that tapped into the public's worries and insecurities. Young men responded in droves, seeking the strength and self-confidence they saw in Earle Liederman. To those who responded to his ads, Earle sent an elaborate, well-illustrated booklet on muscular development, featuring photos of his best students along with testimonials and an explanation about his techniques and philosophy. In the seventh edition of the booklet, Earle shows several photographs of his best and most admired student, Charles Atlas. Not surprisingly, the Earle Liederman Mail-Order Course and the Charles Atlas Dynamic Tension Course are virtually the same in the methods employed. Atlas's course, however, uses no form of resistance other than your own body while Liederman has a few exercises with the chest expander.

Liederman's course was primarily *free hand*, with a strong emphasis on the push-up as the key to phenomenal upper body strength and development, and the single leg knee bend as the key to lower body development. He also encouraged students to do a wide variety of chinning exercises, although he never gave specific recommendations for sets and repetitions. Yet he did seem to favor one set of 6-8 repetitions on most of his other exercises (with the exception of push-ups and deep knee bends).

For the push-up, I quote Liederman from his *12 Week Bodybuilding Course*, Lesson 7: "Try for a record in the floor dipping or push-up, at least once a week. See how many times you can do it with your feet on the floor, or in other words, in the easier manner. I have done it 101 times without resting. I simply mention this to show you what patient practice will do. By the time you can do it 73-100 times without resting, you will have a wonderful chest development—not to speak of fine triceps."

Then in the last paragraph of the same lesson, Liederman says the following: "Another way to try for a record and strength test in the push-up is to have someone push down on your head or between your shoulders while you are lying on your stomach on the floor, and then try to push up. After a while, you can have someone sit on your shoulders and push up. If you can do this twice, you are very good, for it is quite a stunt."

From Good Times to the Great Depression

Throughout the 1920s, Liederman succeeded in a huge way. His course sold for $32 in 1920, which today is the equivalent of $324. He became a millionaire several times over with a fleet of expensive sports cars, a beauty queen for a wife, and all the other trappings of success. Although Earle was the embodiment of the American Dream during the 1920s, his charmed life and glorious prosperity came to a crashing halt in October 1929 when the stock market took a dive. By early 1930 he had lost *everything*, including Miss Beauty Queen.

Yet, no matter what kind of adversity struck, Earle always managed to land on his feet. During the 1930s, he got a job as a radio host on a New Jersey exercise program and was a hit with female listeners. That was partly because he would often read poetry on the air between workouts, thus proving to his audience that he was every bit as sensitive as he was strong and handsome.

During the 1940s, a former pupil convinced Liederman to move to Hollywood. There he found work writing for a quiz show, but his main interest remained bodybuilding. Then when Joe Weider was searching for an editor for a new publication, it was Earle who got the job. *Weider's Muscle Power* first appeared in 1945, and it was a hit almost from the beginning due to his direction.

In his later years, Earle became a born-again Christian and devoted his entire life to his newfound faith. He was completing a book on religious faith at the time of his death in 1970.

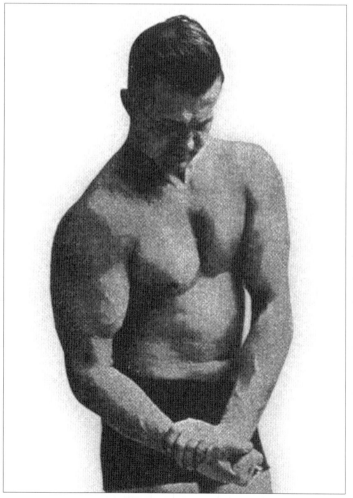

CHARLES ATLAS
THE MAN, THE LEGEND

"Do not go where the path may lead, go instead where there is no path and leave a trail."

—RALPH WALDO EMERSON

It starts with a beating you get on the way home from a Halloween party. A thug beats you senseless until you fall unconscious, and there's nothing you can do about it except go home and cry and ask God to help you find a way to become strong. Then with a steely resolve, you go to the YMCA the next day and try to get strong by lifting weights. And you keep going day after day. But you're so skinny and weak it just seems to wear you out.

Yet you won't give up. For inspiration, you go to the Brooklyn Museum of Art and study the sculptures of beautifully muscled Grecian athletes. While you dream of someday looking just as they do, perfectly developed from head to toe, you remind yourself of how terrible that beating felt, and you vow to never let it happen again.

Eight months pass, and you're at the beach with a beautiful girl lying at your side. You're having a great time until the local bully shows up. He steps in front of you and asks your girl why she's with such a scrawny guy,

and then the big ox kicks sand in your face. First, he insults you, then he humiliates you—but once again, there's nothing you can do about it . . . except take it. Or is there?

Angelo Siciliano Transformed

Everything I've recounted so far really did happen to a sixteen-year-old young man by the name of Angelo Siciliano. And there was nothing he could do about it. He couldn't even write to Charles Atlas as did millions of other young men over the next fifty years. No, he couldn't write to Charles Atlas because there was no Charles Atlas at the time.

So Angelo went to his favorite place, the Brooklyn Zoo, to be alone and to think about his dilemma. He ended up in the section where the big jungle cats were housed. Lions and tigers and even a beautiful black panther were there, and as he watched them, he got a revelation. The giant cats didn't use barbells and dumbbells or any other apparatus. They just stretched their muscles with great tension when they changed positions and paced back and forth. Yet the cats had beautiful muscles that rippled like waves beneath their fur whenever they moved.

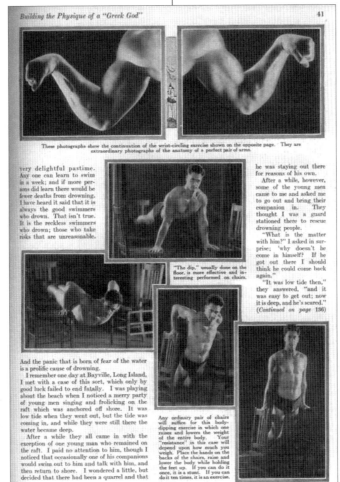

Physical Culture Magazine, Dec. 1921

Angelo wondered what would happen if a human being did the same thing. So he went home and started experimenting, and sure enough it WORKED! Before long he was packing on pound after pound of solid muscle. Then he added hundreds of push-ups, sit-ups, and deep knee bends to his newfound physical training system. Before long he started doing the same hand-balancing feats he saw the acrobats at Coney Island doing.

Soon all his friends as well as several young ladies noticed that Angelo, whom they'd nicknamed "Charlie," had transformed himself into the most beautifully developed young athlete any of them had ever seen. In fact, after another day at the beach, Angelo and his buddies were walking home when one of them stopped, pointed to the statue in front of the Atlas Hotel, and said, "Hey, Charlie, you look even better than that Atlas guy."

This statement stopped him in his tracks . . . and transformed his life. Born on October 30, 1893, in Calabria, the southernmost province of Italy, and having emigrated to the United States at the age of ten with his family, Angelo Siciliano decided to change his name. And that name, Charles Atlas, became the stuff of legends. Barely twenty-one years old, he embarked on a destiny that forever changed and continues to change the lives of millions of young men and women.

Charles Atlas Meets Earle E. Liederman

Charles Atlas decided to open his own strong man act on Coney Island in 1915 at the age of twenty-two. At virtually every performance and demonstration he noted many young men who wanted to know what they could do to transform their physiques to look like his. Then, in 1917, he met Earle E. Liederman. The two men decided to put together a vaudeville act that showcased their strength, hand-balancing skills, and physical development. They toured America and were phenomenally popular, selling out theaters across the country.

In 1919, Liederman decided to settle down and promote a mail-order bodybuilding course. In fact, in the early editions of his "Muscular Development" promotional brochure (late 1919), Liederman included several photos of Charles Atlas, making reference to Charles as his most outstanding pupil. Obviously, it worked to Liederman's advantage to say that the Atlas physique was the result of his training system, but it was not completely true. After all, before the two men met, Atlas was already exceptionally well developed. What is true, though, is that they did spend many hours training together, and there is no doubt they utilized the same training method. Their respective bodybuilding courses are virtually identical with the exception that Liederman's course included the use of an elastic chest expander while Atlas's

Physical Culture Magazine, Dec. 1921

course was completely comprised of free-hand movements.

Charles Atlas Meets Charles Roman

The two men went their separate ways in 1920. Atlas worked as an artist model and opened a gym where he taught his methods while Earle became the king of mail-order bodybuilders. In both 1921 and 1922, Charles Atlas won the title, "The World's Most Perfectly Developed Man." He took his prize money and endeavored to emulate Earle's success with a mail-order bodybuilding course of his own. From 1922 to 1929, he was only moderately successful. But in 1929 that all changed when he took Charles Roman on as his business partner. Almost from the moment they began together, they were incredibly successful, which was due primarily to Roman's keen promotional skill and knack for creating the Charles Atlas legend and keeping Atlas in the public eye. Despite the Great Depression of the 1930s, the two men became millionaires.

From the 1930s to the 1950s, a large number of famous people became students of Charles Atlas. The list includes John F. Kennedy,

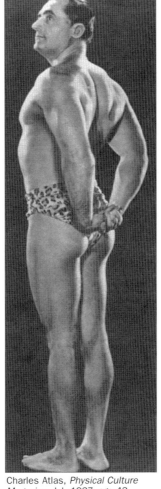

Charles Atlas, *Physical Culture Magazine*, July 1937, age 43

boxers Joe Louis and Rocky Marciano, Robert L. Ripley (of *Ripley's Believe It or Not*), New York Yankee Joe DiMaggio, and even Mahatma Ghandi. It is reported that when one of the young ladies who opened the mail brought Gandhi's letter to Charles Roman, he immediately took it to Charles Atlas and asked, "What should we charge him?" According to the story, Atlas told Roman, "Just send him the whole thing at no charge. The poor little fella is just a bag of bones."

In addition to keeping Atlas in the public eye through news articles and magazine advertising, Roman had Atlas on a large number of television programs throughout the 1950s and 1960s. That all changed in 1965 when the love of Charles Atlas's life, his wife Margaret, died. At that point, Atlas lost interest in the business, sold his half to Roman, and moved to Florida, where he spent his remaining days until he passed on to be with his beloved shortly after Christmas 1972.

In terms of impact, I doubt that anyone has ever done as much as Charles Atlas to elevate the public's perception of manly strength. To this day his name remains a synonym for strength, determination, and the guts to fight back.

"The secret of health for both mind and body
is not to mourn for the past, not to worry
about the future, or not to anticipate troubles,
but to live in the present moment
wisely and earnestly."

— Author Unknown

WOODY STRODE

BODY SCULPTED BY MICHELANGELO

"Only those who will risk going too far can possibly find out how far one can go."

—T. S. ELIOT

Have you ever seen the movie *Spartacus*? If you haven't, your first assignment is to check your local television logs and watch it. Or, better yet, go to the video store and rent it. Either way, you're in for one of the greatest movies ever made. In fact, *Spartacus* is often ranked as the #1 manliest film of all time. Having watched it many times, I agree with that ranking. Besides featuring a young, muscular Kirk Douglas (who trained using Dynamic Tension) in the lead role of Spartacus, it also has incredible performances by Sir Laurence Olivier, Charles Laughton, Tony Curtis, Jean Simmons, and Woody Strode, who played a pivotal role in the film although he was never given marquee credit.

Woody in 1948 at the beginning of his pro wrestling career.

Woody Strode was born in 1914 in Los Angeles and grew up under the shadow of segregation with all its accompanying disadvantages. However, Woody was gifted with extraordinary physical abilities and became one of the first black athletes to break into professional football. That came after having enjoyed a stellar career catching passes as a left end for the UCLA football team and having proven himself as a world-class track and field athlete.

In his book, *Goal Dust*, Woody relates several phenomenal stories, one of which involved modeling for two paintings that had been commissioned by, of all people, Adolf Hitler in 1936. This happened just prior to the 1936 Olympic Games in Berlin, when Woody says that Leni Riefenstahl, Hitler's filmmaker of the *Triumph of the Will* and *Olympiad*, contacted him about filming him. She said, "We'd like to take you up to Carmel and film you against that beautiful white scenery." He also quotes Riefenstahl who told him that this was Hitler's and her reaction to seeing photos of Woody: "We saw your pictures and couldn't believe it. You have the greatest physique of any athlete we have ever seen." Woody goes on to say, "I've often thought that if Hitler had won the war, they would have picked me up and either bred me or dissected me."

Although he was certain he would have had his shot at Olympic gold in the 1940 Helsinki Games, it never happened. Both the 1940 and 1944 Olympics were cancelled due to World War II, during which time Woody enlisted. After the war, he participated in two professional sports—pro wrestling and pro football—and he was a natural star at both. Next came Hollywood and a long and distinguished career in films such as *Sergeant Rutledge, Spartacus, The Professionals,* and many others. Every movie showcased his incredible physique that looked as though Michelangelo had sculpted it.

So how did Woody Strode create the famed physique that even John Wayne said was the most perfectly developed he'd ever seen? Woody tells us on page 42 of *Goal Dust*: "I picked up twenty pounds by doing one thousand push-ups a day. The school didn't allow us to lift weights. The coaches thought weightlifting would slow you down. So I developed natural strength from working out with my own body weight. I got so I could do a thousand push-ups, a thousand sit-ups, and a thousand knee squats every day. With the push-ups, I'd have to rest after every one hundred. The others I could do without stopping. I got into the knee squats because of a wrestler named Gama. He was an Indian wrestler who built this tremendous body by doing five thousand knee squats continuously. It would go on so long they would serve him tea."

There you have it. No weights, no machines, yet Woody Strode had one of the finest bodies ever created by God or man.

From *Sergeant Rutledge* – 1960. Woody was the star but not given marquee credit.

27

ROCKY MARCIANO
THE ORIGINAL "ROCK"

"And in the end, it's not the years in your life that count. It's the life in your years."

—AUTHOR UNKNOWN

When you think of the world's heavyweight boxing champion, you may think of Lennox Lewis, Evander Holyfield, or even Muhammad Ali. And, true enough, all of these men have been great champions. (Please note: I'm saying they are great boxing champions. I'm not saying that these champions are men of great character.)

But there was one heavyweight boxing champion who won the title on September 23, 1952, who was clearly in a class all his own. I'm referring to Rocky Marciano, the man whom virtually all the World War II veterans referred to respectfully as "The Rock."

"The Rock" was born on September 1, 1923. He came up the hard way. Though he was blessed with natural physical talent and was adept at

A happy warrior at the peak of his career.

several sports, it was boxing where he was without equal. His talent was discovered while serving in the U.S. Army during World War II, when he fought numerous exhibition bouts. Within a year and a half of the war ending in September 1945, the then twenty-three-year-old Marciano had his first professional fight on March 17, 1947, against Lee Epperson, whom he KO'd in the third round. The rest is history. During the next five and one half years, "The Rock" took on all comers, including Roland La Starza, Rex Layne, the former champion of the world, legendary Joe Louis (whom he

also KO'd), and Harry Matthews, whom he KO'd on July 28, 1952, less than two months before his title shot against champion Jersey Joe Walcott. How many fighters today would even dare to go in the ring less than 2 months before his title fight.

"The Rock" Vs. Jersey Joe Walcott

The championship shot with Walcott arrived on September 23, 1952. At the weigh-in, "The Rock" was both shorter (5'10-1/2") and lighter (184 pounds). In fact, he was so ripped, he almost looked like a middleweight instead of a heavyweight. From the opening bell, Marciano had his work cut out for him. In fact, he was floored for the first time in his entire career during his first round with Jersey Joe.

If you stop and think about it, most men would have given up or been totally intimidated at that point. But not "The Rock." He immediately got up and pursued the attack. However, no matter how hard he pursued, it looked as though Jersey Joe was going to give him "The Butt Kicking" of a lifetime, which, in fact, he did.

A fact about this fight that is sometimes overlooked is that Rocky was blinded for several of the middle rounds of the fight, similar to the way Muhammad Ali was blinded in his first fight with Sonny Liston. In the sixth round the combatants accidentally butted heads, opening a cut atop Rocky's head. His corner put medication on the wound to stop the bleeding. And possibly it was this that ran down into his eyes. Others at ringside felt Walcott's people had put something on Walcott's gloves or shoulder to blind Marciano. To quote "The Rock" after the fight, "It seemed like Walcott had some stuff between his neck and shoulder where I rested my head when we got in close. Every time we came together, my eyes would start smarting again."

Whatever the source, Marciano was almost completely blind for three rounds and took a terrible beating. Promoter Sam Silverman was quoted as saying, "Walcott had the legs of a twenty-year-old. He was having the best fight of his career. He must've put Rocky into two hundred head-on collisions. It was one of the worst lickings I ever seen a guy get."

Rocky's own friend, Nicky Sylvester, was asked by a reporter, "What's happening to your pal?" Nicky's reply was, "What do you think is happening? He's getting his brains knocked out." Still another friend by the name of Izzy Gold was quoted as saying, "I'll never forget it. Rocky was taking one incredible pounding."

In his book, *Who Was the Greatest*, author Richard B. Stockton wrote, "He was almost helpless, and Walcott opened up in an effort to end the fight. Rocky took a beating in those rounds, but plodded on." To put it bluntly, it was one of the most amazing displays of courage and determination ever shown in the ring or anywhere else. Except for one crushing right to the jaw in the tenth round, Rocky had been unable to land a solid punch. And as he stalked the wily champion, battering his arms and body with sledgehammer-like blows, he bled from eye cuts and a deep, ugly gash on the bridge of the nose.

By the twelfth round Rocky was hopelessly behind on points. He knew he was losing, and one thought kept burning through his mind: "I've got to KO him to win. Just one shot—that's all I need."

What Rocky really needed was a miracle at that stage. All Walcott had to do was stay away from him and coast for three more rounds. Jersey Joe had the fight won on all the official score cards, and he was about to snap Rocky's string of 37 knockouts in 42 straight wins.

Although it took 13 rounds and the "butt kicking" of his lifetime to take the title from Jersey Joe, it took "The Rock" less than a round to defend it.

And then, with explosive suddenness, the miracle happened. As Jersey Joe faded against the rope, trying to sucker in Marciano, "The Rock" loosed a shattering right to the jaw. The 40,379 fans in Philadelphia's Municipal Stadium gasped in stunned disbelief as champion Walcott slumped to the canvas. The referee then began the slow count to ten. In reality, he could have counted to 100 because Walcott was out. One sportswriter captured the scene in these words: "You could see his body quiver with shock. His lips, cheeks, nose and eyes all seemed to shake loose and run together like blobs of wet mud, then he sank. Slowly, painfully, pathetically. When he fluttered to the canvas, he had no more life than a rag doll." Jersey Joe himself put it more succinctly: "Soon as it landed, the lights went out."

What Made "The Rock" so Powerful?

So what does "The Rock" have to do with your personal transformation or how it relates to the "Push-up" as the cornerstone of your upper body strength and conditioning program. I can answer that in one word. *Everything.* I give you three key points.

Number 1. In almost all his professional fights, "The Rock" had to fight bigger men than himself. All were taller. Some were heavier. Though none were stronger. Or for that matter, as strong.

Number 2. Virtually everyone with half a brain who has ever viewed Marciano's first championship fight acknowledges, as did his opponent, that "The Rock" was pound for pound the strongest, best-conditioned fighter in history. If you think that's a stretch, go to a video store and rent a copy of the Marciano/Walcott championship fights. Then observe that in the first of the two fights "The Rock" is constantly throwing punches in hot pursuit, even though he is getting a royal butt kicking. Then watch as in the thirteenth round he lets go with a single shattering right to the jaw. That's it. One punch that practically takes Walcott's head off. One punch! Not a combination. Again, remind yourself. Rocky did that after getting his butt kicked for twelve rounds.

Number 3. Charles Atlas was proud to point to Rocky Marciano as a perfect example of what his "Dynamic Tension Training System" could do to give a man off-the-charts phenomenal strength and punching power.

In fact, it was push-ups that Rocky did hundreds of each day that gave him the stamina and punching power to hit his specially made heavy bag that weighed 300 pounds instead of the standard 200-pound bags his opponents were using. Figure it out. If a guy is strong enough to hit a 300-pound heavy bag for fifteen 3-minute rounds, how hard do you think he could hit a 220-pound man? Enough said.

"It is not the critic who counts;
not the man who points out how the strong man stumbled
or where the doer of deeds could have done them better.
The credit belongs to the man
who is actually in the arena,
whose face is marred by dust and sweat and blood;
who strives valiantly;
who errs and comes short again and again;
who knows great enthusiasms,
the great devotions;
who spends himself in a worthy cause;
who at the best, knows in the end the triumph of high achievement,
and who, at the worst, if he fails, at least fails while
DARING GREATLY
so that his place shall never be
with those timid souls
who know neither victory or defeat."

— Theodore Roosevelt

HERSCHEL WALKER
A SUPERSTAR'S APPROACH TO SUPER STRENGTH AND CONDITIONING

"To be nobody-but-yourself—in a world which is doing its best night and day, to make you everybody else—means to fight the hardest battle which any human being can fight; and never stop fighting."

—E. E. CUMMINGS

If you study his statistics, it's undeniable. Counting his USFL stats, Herschel Walker leads pro football running backs in nearly every category. Plus, he is the only man in NFL history to have a 90+ yard play rushing, receiving, and on special teams all in the same year. Despite posting remarkable numbers, perhaps the most surprising statistic is that in only one of his NFL years did he average more than twenty carries per game. That came in 1988, Tom Landry's last year in Dallas, when Herschel led the NFL with 1500+ yards on a horrible Cowboy's team that had few other offensive weapons. He was then traded to the Minnesota Vikings, a team that had no way to utilize or maximize his talents. Later he played with the Philadelphia Eagles, the New York Giants, and ended his career playing for the Cowboys.

Looking back over his NFL career, there are a few facts that stand out as exceptional and tell us something special about the man. Consider this: Walker is one of the very few running backs who was as productive *after* his first five years as he was during them. Then think about this: he was one of the least injured running backs in NFL history, despite the fact that he never played on a championship team with an offensive line that could protect him. What was his secret?

It was due in no small part to the fact that at 6'1" and 225 pounds, Walker was by far the best conditioned athlete in the entire NFL, which was widely acknowledged by his peers at the time. And how do you suppose this incredible athlete achieved his legendary fitness? Would you believe by utilizing a program that is almost a carbon copy of Woody Strode's?

In his book *Basic Training*, Herschel made it clear that he did not weight train with barbells, dumbbells, or machines. His entire program consisted of push-ups (all variations—hand stand, close arm, wide arm, standard, one arm, weighted), chins (multiple variations), sit-ups, sprints, and pulling a tractor tire from a rope tied around his waist while running uphill. Even as recently as the July 15, 2002 issue of *Sports Illustrated*, it was reported that the forty-year-old Herschel still performs 1,500 push-ups and 3,000 sit-ups each day. Yes, you read that right—each day. That was the secret to his success then and now.

Which brings up a point for you to consider seriously. Herschel Walker is a multimillionaire who can easily afford a completely equipped gym. But instead he chooses to continue to use the tried, true, and proven program that made him the best conditioned athlete in the NFL and an exemplary superstar. I want to encourage you that you can realize your ultimate God-given potential by training in an entirely natural method such as is found in this book, and it doesn't have to cost you a fortune to do it.

MATT FUREY

I SAVED THE BEST FOR LAST

"Life is not a 'brief candle.' It is a splendid torch that I want to make burn as brightly as possible before handing on to future generations."

—GEORGE BERNARD SHAW

If I lived another lifetime, what I owe Matt Furey could never be repaid. Because of him, I have attained the highest level of all-around strength and fitness in my life. And, believe me, that's saying a lot. But before I tell you about his impact on my life, I first need to tell this incredible man's story and his many accomplishments.

Matt Furey grew up in Carroll, Iowa. Almost from birth he showed the desire to excel in athletics—yet in the early going his talent was "average." He began competing in both swimming and wrestling at the age of eight and eventually became a champion in both sports. The fact that he chose these sports at such an early age tells you something about the uniqueness of the man. Although swimming and wrestling are both technically *team* sports in that the performance of each *individual* impacts the overall team score, they are nonetheless individual sports where each individual competes solely on his own merits. Winning or losing are up to the individual. To become a champion at either sport puts you in that elite class of athletes who possess the drive and tenacity to demand of themselves what no one else, be it a coach or a trainer, could possibly demand.

In high school Matt was the Iowa 3A State Runner-up at 167 pounds. From 1981 to 1984 he attended the University of Iowa where he wrestled and was coached by the famed Olympic Gold Medallist Dan Gable. In the fall of 1984 he transferred to Edinboro University of Pennsylvania, and in 1985 he won the NCAA II national wrestling title at 167 pounds. In 1987 he opened a personal training

business for wrestlers and fitness enthusiasts whom he trained one-on-one.

In 1990 Matt decided to round out his martial skills and began studying other martial arts in addition to wrestling, at which he was already champion caliber. Immediately he saw the physical, mental, and philosophical links these arts had with wrestling. This led directly to the publication of his breakthrough book and video series entitled *The Martial Art of Wrestling.*

"If you want to learn 'Catch' wrestling, Matt's the Man."
—J.P.

In 1996 the competition bug bit once again, and Matt began competing in a style of grappling known as Shuai-Chiao, which is the oldest form of kung fu. Furey's teacher, Dr. Daniel Weng, a national champion from Taiwan and a ninth-degree black belt, guided Furey to three national titles in the art. Then, during Christmas 1997, Matt was part of Dr. Weng's U.S. delegation competing in the World Kung Fu Shuai-Chiao tournament in Beijing, China. Furey took home the coveted Gold Medal in the 90 KG (198 pounds) class and was the only non-Chinese combatant to win a title. In addition, his win was historic because it marked the *only* time an American had *ever* won a *gold* medal in any martial arts competition held in China.

Matt continued his personal training business, which was very successful. But in April 1999, he met Karl Gotch, who forever change Matt's life. Gotch was a 1948 Olympian from Belgium and had been known as "The God of Pro Wrestling in Japan" for over 20 years. He was the world's foremost authority on the lost art of Catch-As-Catch-Can Wrestling. Matt was so impressed with Gotch's knowledge of conditioning and catch-as-catch-can that he moved his wife, Zhannie, and son, Frank, to Tampa, Florida, so he could learn from Gotch firsthand.

In spite of his national and world titles, and fully believing that he already knew everything about strength and conditioning, Matt says, "Karl helped me understand that my 36-year-old body, a body that many people considered to be highly athletic was, in fact, stiff, weak, and in many ways non-functional." Within a short period of time, Matt could hardly believe how his strength, endurance, and flexibility all took a big leap forward—solely by using the body-weight exercise method as taught by Gotch. Matt then realized that the entire Western world had been sold a bill of goods as regards strength and conditioning that simply wasn't true. In February 2000, Matt published his groundbreaking bestseller, *Combat Conditioning*, in which he revealed the exact methods taught to him by Karl Gotch.

Almost from the day it was released, *Combat Conditioning* turned the entire world of strength and physical conditioning on its ear. Some self-proclaimed experts tried in vain to discredit Furey's methods, but a strange phenomena happened. People all over the world began achieving levels of strength and fitness they never dreamed possible, no matter what training method they had previously employed. And then something else happened. People who had been injured due to incorrect training methods suddenly discovered that their bodies began to heal while using the *Combat Conditioning* exercises.

Which brings the story back to me. In June 1988, I was helping a friend prepare for an upcoming martial arts tournament. I was 36 years old and in phenomenal shape. It was during an all-out sparring session that my friend Mark threw a spinning side kick. I saw it come and threw a reverse block to the outside with my left arm. I threw it with such force that it actually knocked him off balance and he fell. But at the moment of impact I felt a strange something happen in my left shoulder. It wasn't exactly pain, but I knew something was terribly wrong. I should have stopped immediately, but I kept on despite knowing it was hurt badly. I didn't know how badly, however, until the next morning when I couldn't even rotate my arm into my shirtsleeve. I went for an appointment with a specialist in sports medicine who told me I needed surgery. I considered it, but decided against it after talking to other men who had had a similar shoulder surgery.

LIKE FATHER LIKE SON *"Frank Furey getting one-on-one training with his dad."*
—J.P.

Then I heard about a chiropractor by the name of Tatianna Rioboken, who had a remarkable success rate in rehabilitating such injuries. She agreed that I had severely injured my left shoulder, and her method of treatment involved the use of electro-acupuncture, which I undertook weekly for a period of several months. My strength began to slowly return, but I was constantly aware of my injury and wanted desperately to totally rehabilitate it to the point it had been prior to the injury. So I searched every day to find a solution, but it would be 12 years later before I found it.

In the fall of 2000 I stumbled upon information about an incredible new exercise method found in a book called *Combat Conditioning*. I went to the Internet and discovered how to contact the publisher, then called and left a message. The next day I got a phone call from Matt Furey himself. He listened patiently as I told him about the injury and asked if his program might help. He said, "Look, John. I don't know how bad the injury is, but I've had people tell me that their old injuries began healing when they started practicing the exercises. About the only downside for you would be that they would have no effect one way or the other."

I could hardly believe it. No hard sell. Just honesty and what sounded like a genuine concern. I immediately ordered the book and asked if Matt would Fed Ex it overnight. Matt laughed and said, "Sure." I must have sounded like a drowning man in need of a life preserver. And in a way I was.

That life preserver arrived the next day, and I'll never forget the first time I tried a Furey Push-up. I was actually afraid of what might happen to my shoulder after all this time (how's that for the body's trauma memory?). I started slowly, and during the downward circular descent I felt my muscles twitching uncontrollably in my left shoulder, but it didn't hurt so I completed one full repetition. Then I did another and another until I reached 7 and decided to stop and wait a while, and try some of his other exercises. When I looked at the Furey Bridge, I couldn't believe it would ever be possible to achieve what I saw him doing in the photos. Then I looked at the cover of his book and saw something that told me to trust him. It was that "Charles Atlas" smile. The one that reassured me when I was ten years old

that I could one day be strong after my battle with polio. And here I was 38 years later seeing it once again in the face of Matt Furey.

So I persisted and within a month I was cranking out 30 Furey Push-ups in a row with *no pain!* Then one night my wife, Denise, asked me, "Honey, do you ever take aspirin anymore?" "What for?" I returned. "Your shoulder." "No, babe. The shoulder doesn't hurt anymore." She looked surprised but didn't say anything more. Then about 6 weeks later, after performing what Matt refers to as "The Royal Court" every morning, I ran into the bedroom and told Denise that I did it! She just smiled and said, "What did you do now?" "I did 100 Furey Push-ups in one continuous set in flawless form and 500 Furey Squats in 18 minutes and 34 seconds. Then I almost touched my nose on the Bridge." She laughed and said that I was like a little kid making an new discovery. Well, she was right. I discovered the way to totally rehabilitate my shoulder and to no longer require *any* pain medication.

"Yes, he's as flexible as he is strong."
—J.P.

I was so excited that I called Matt's office to tell him of my results (and because I wanted to order everything else he had available). I received a return call from Matt's staff telling me that Matt was out of town but would contact me very soon as he was very interested in my story. To my surprise I got a call from Matt the next day and we spoke for over an hour. It wasn't until later that I found out (from Matt's brother) that Matt is a very private person who rarely makes a phone call to anyone—and this includes some famous celebrities who have tried to get a hold of him for private training, all to no avail. One day, some months later, I asked Matt why he had taken me under his wing and given me so much of his time. He quickly replied: "Very few people know this about me, and I hope you don't take this to be sort of whacky, but I'm a metaphysical kind of guy, and I had a feeling deep in my gut that I am supposed to be talking to you." He said nothing more and I didn't ask, but over time I came to know exactly what he meant. After that day Matt introduced me to many of his other close friends through something he called his Inner Circle. Each day I found out what the other members were up to. We quickly became a brotherhood of like-minded individuals. Anything with regards to training and self-improvement was open for discussion. What amazed me the most was that my complete rehab was not at all the *exception*. It seemed to be the norm. Countless others, some with injuries far worse than mine, told about the effectiveness of the Furey training methods to rehab their injuries.

So there you have it. Now you know why I have such a high level of respect and appreciation for Matt Furey. Not only did I totally regain my shoulder but I found myself doing feats I never imagined possible. For instance, I ordered Matt and his friend Ed Baran's course called "The Secret Power of Handstand Training"—a perfectly written instruction manual and video instruction tape. At the beginning of the video, Matt performs a handstand between two standard dining room chairs with seats 18" from the floor. He descended slowly into an Extended Range Handstand Push-up until his head touched the carpet, then he paused and slowly pushed himself back up to full extension. That would be a great feat of strength for a 155-pound gymnast, but from a guy who weighs 220, it's in the realm of dreams. Needless to say it motivated me, and now at age 50 I routinely perform this exercise almost daily. In addition to the wide range of other books and courses from Matt, he has also produced what I believe is the preeminent work on strength, athletic development, and physical culture called Gama Fitness. It is truly an outstanding investment worth many times its price.

"Matt Furey, The Living Personification of Strength and Athletic Fitness." (P.S. Don't try this at home)
—J.P.

If you want to purchase any of the Matt Furey line of products, you may do so via the Internet by going directly to **www.mattfurey.com**. From my perspective, you can't go wrong in doing so.

"Now that you've met some of my heroes, it's time to take a serious look at how you can transform yourself into one, with Transformetrics™."

—J.P.

"Man often becomes what he believes him-self to be. If I keep on saying to myself that I cannot do a certain thing, it is possible that I may end by really becoming inca-pable of doing it. On the contrary, if I shall have the belief I can do it, I shall surely acquire the capacity to do it, even if I may not have it at the beginning."

—MAHATMA GANDHI,
Indian Nationalist Leader (1869-1948)

On the pages that follow I will outline my complete *Transformetrics™ Training System*. I have divided it into twelve consecutive lessons just as Charles Atlas and Earle E. Liederman did with their legendary courses. In it you will find every-thing necessary to develop every muscle in your body from your neck to your toes and according to your body's natural perfection. You will be awed by the remarkable increases you will achieve in *all* facets of true dynamic functional strength and fitness, although it will be most

evident in the transformation of your physique. The lithe, hard musculature your body will assume and the phenomenal increase in your strength-to-body-weight ratio will have to be seen to be believed.

How I Created TRANSFORMETRICS™

As I stated in the Introduction, I began training at the age of ten, after getting the stuffing knocked out of me by a bully three times my size. To say that I was highly motivated when my grandfather and Uncle Wally put me on a hybrid program of the Atlas and Liederman training sys-tems is a monumental understatement. The results I achieved were fantastic, mainly because I had such excellent mentors. But I didn't stop there! I have constantly researched and integrat-ed new and better methods of training in my own *Transformetrics™* system.

The Criteria for the Creation of TRANSFORMETRICS™

■ *Results!* That's the bottom line. When it comes to strength, all-around good health, radiant energy, youthfulness, and well-being, I don't have time for delayed gratification. I can tell you with absolute certainty that every *Transformetrics™* exercise is here because it's among *the best of the best*. There's only so much time in any given day, and it's silly to waste any of it on exercises that don't produce *maximum results!*

■ The *main focus* of the exercises selected has been physique development (muscle building) plus maximization of all seven attributes of dynamic athletic fitness, injury prevention, and complete body rejuvenation. This means that by following this training system you won't be destroying your joints, compressing your spine, draining your energy, or prematurely aging yourself. To the contrary, you will feel energized to the max and every area of your life will be enhanced.

■ *No equipment required.* With the exception of a bar or tree branch to chin yourself, dipping bars, and chairs, no other equipment of any kind is required or necessary. In fact, *you don't even need these* to create the kind of strength and fitness I present. As you will soon discover, there are over 100 exercises to choose from that will do the job beautifully. The reason I included these exercises is because I have personally practiced various types of chins and dips and know from experience that they are great exercises for teaching your muscles to work together in groups, thus maximizing athletic fitness. That said, every other exercise requires no equipment and can be performed while sitting, standing, or lying down (as with crunches). This allows you to exercise virtually anytime and anywhere, making it ideal for people who can't get to a gym, military personnel, students, or busy travelers. In fact, it's perfect for anyone who wants a great body without

having to rely on anything other than *one's own body.*

■ *Time.* I'm a busy man. There are a lot of things I want to do in life. For that reason I have always exercised in a way that would get the job done in 45 minutes or less if I choose to do it in one session a day. Or better still, one that I could break up in segments I could do in 10 minutes or less through the day, focusing on maximum attention and energy on each exercise.

■ *Variation.* Each chapter or lesson focuses primarily on one muscle group at a time—neck, shoulders, chest, back, arms, forearms, abdomen, legs (upper and lower)—and each muscle group is exercised from a wide variety of angles and directions through a full range of movement, resulting in the most complete and functional development possible.

■ *Effectiveness!* Many people find it hard to believe that I have attained and maintain my level of strength and development without ever using weights or machines. This is because most people have been told by the propagandists of exercise literature (most of whom are in the business of selling exercise equipment or are paid by them for advertising space) that it is impossible to attain great development without either weights or machines. Take a look at my pictures and reread the success profiles, especially on Woody Strode, Herschel Walker, and Matt Furey. The fact is your muscles respond to tension, and it make no difference how that tension is applied. You can use the *Transformetrics*™ exercises to develop and maintain a beautiful musculature while at the same time developing a level of concentration that allows your mind and body to become one. Once you have achieved that, you won't want to train any other way, because you will have become the master of your own destiny.

The types of exercises in my *Transformetrics™ Training System* are divided into four distinct categories: Isometric Contractions, Isotonics, Joint Mobility and Flexibility, and Aerobic.

1. Isometric Contractions

People who don't know any better often say that Charles Atlas's training system was made up of isometric exercises. Anytime I hear or read that statement I know that the so-called expert doesn't know what he or she is talking about. In truth, I can't think of a single "true" isometric exercise that was part of the Atlas regimen.

So what exactly is a *true* isometric exercise? It is an exercise that strengthens a particular muscle by tightening it, holding it, and then relaxing, all without moving the joint. For my purposes, isometric contractions are exercises that utilize *ultra-high tension* in fixed positions against an immovable object or resistance. For instance, try standing in a doorway with your palms at approximately shoulder height and pushing outward with all your might for 10 or more seconds while breathing out making an "ssss" sound like air being let of a tire. (Be careful: if you're as strong as Samson, the whole place might come down on top of you.) This exercise creates tremendous tension as the muscles try to contract with near maximal force, but there is no discernible movement.

When applied in a wide variety of positions, isometrics can dramatically increase strength and enhance muscular definition to a point that is

hard to imagine. However, in order to achieve the best possible results with isometrics, they need to be incorporated into a training system with full range movement exercises (otherwise, you will be ultra-strong at only certain fixed positions) just as they are in my *Transformetrics™ Training System*.

Men who have successfully implemented isometrics into their training systems and achieved spectacular results include Alexander Zass, whose stage name was Samson during the 1920s. Zass was famous for bending iron bars and breaking chains. He was said to have developed his phenomenal strength when he was a prisoner of war in World War I, exercising isometrically against cell bars and chains.

During the 1960s and early 1970s, martial arts legend Bruce Lee used isometrics both to increase his strength and to create his signature muscular definition. Those who knew him personally said that after he severely injured his lower back with a weight training exercise called the Good Morning, where you bend forward to a right angle with a barbell across your shoulders, Bruce began using isometrics to the point of fanaticism. This is partly due to the fact that after the weight-training accident, Lee never lived another day without severe back pain. Hence, he needed a reliable alternative training method, which turned out to be isometrics.

In more contemporary times, isometrics have been championed by Matt Furey in his world famous Gama Fitness Training System (to check it out, go to www.mattfurey.com). In Gama Fitness, Matt gives by far the most exhaustive, detailed, and comprehensive program of exercises I have seen for using isometrics to develop superhuman strength and power from every direction and angle. As Matt says, "The possibilities are limitless."

The only drawback to isometrics that I can even remotely see is the fact that you have to have a laser-like focused mind control over your muscles

in order to make them contract as maximally as possible. But on second thought, that is not really a drawback, it's a tremendous plus. And I'm not just referring to isometric exercises either, but to harnessing this ability in all areas of your life.

2. Isotonic Exercises

Isotonic exercise is any exercise where actual movement is required. Calisthenics, gymnastics, weightlifting, swimming, and running are all examples of isotonic exercises. However, for our purposes we are going to break isotonic exercises into three distinct categories:

Group 1: Power Calisthenics (PC). These are body weight exercises that allow you to develop your body from a wide variety of angles and directions. They are not the garden variety of calisthenics that are little more than twisting and turning. To the contrary, there are several that would challenge even the world's strongest athletes, such as the "One Arm Furey Push-up" or the "Extended Range Handstand Push-up" between chairs. I learned both of these from Matt Furey.

Group 2: Dynamic Self-Resistance (DSR). This was the mainstay of the Atlas, Liederman, MacFadden, and Maxick training systems. Call it whatever you want, but we're talking about a method where one muscle group acts as resistance for another. These exercises can be very vigorous, taxing even the strongest of men. The secret is deep concentration as one limb acts as resistance for another while allowing a full range of motion to occur. If isometric stops are incorporated into these exercises (usually at the beginning, mid range, and end), it is possible to completely exhaust each muscle group within 3-5 repetitions.

Group 3: Dynamic Visualized Resistance (DVR). First, watch yourself in a mirror as you do the following. Step 1. With you arm at your side, palm facing up, bend your arm at the elbow and bring your palm and fingers in close proximity to your shoulders. No big deal, right? Okay, now try it this way. Step 2. Once again, begin with your arm at your side, palm up. First, clench your fist as tight as possible. Pretend you are gripping a 100-pound dumbbell so hard your knuckles are turning white. Then slowly bend at the elbow with flawless form and curl your fist to your shoulder, feeling the muscles of your forearm and upper arm contracting with maximal force as you slowly raise the imaginary dumbbell throughout the

entire range of motion. Don't be surprised if the muscles shake or vibrate. If you do it correctly, your muscles will contract with the same intensity as though you really were lifting a heavy dumbbell. This is what is meant by *Dynamic Visualized Resistance*. You literally visualize you are working against an imaginary heavy resistance. In addition to the type of exercise just mentioned above, you can use this method to add resistance to calisthenic strength exercises of all types, such as push-ups, pull-ups, sit-ups, and all forms of strength training.

The key is to maintain laser-like focused mind control and to think into the muscles as you work them. This was the strength training strategy of martial arts legend John McSweeney. John's martial art and physical culture systems were second to none. He taught a system of seven Dynamic Visualized Resistance Exercises that he called "Tiger Moves." John himself had a powerfully developed physique that most people would have assumed was the result of years of heavy weight training, but in reality John *never* touched weights and proved both through himself and his students that his "Tiger Moves" exercises were vastly superior for body conditioning and lifelong strength and youthfulness.

Bottom line: If you can develop the laser-like mind over muscles focus necessary, you can use it to develop your body to perfection with little else required.

3. Joint Mobility and Flexibility

These exercises allow you to maintain youthful flexibility and agility without the worry of injury. They are easy to do and offer immediate feedback to inform you if any part of your body is stiff, sore, or injured. These exercises are vitally important to your health and well-being and are used to warm-up and stretch before you do the *Transformetrics™ Strength Exercises*. Even if you don't have time to do the strength training on any given day, I still want you to do these.

Believe me, these exercises alone are worth the price of this book.

4. Aerobic Exercises

In 1968, Dr. Kenneth Cooper created an entirely new category of exercise—aerobics. The key to health and fitness, Dr. Cooper theorized, was in the body's ability to process oxygen into the bloodstream. In general, it is any exercise that can be continued for 20 minutes or longer at an intensity level that allows for a cardiovascular training effect. The most popular aerobic exercises include running, swimming, cycling, rowing, and power walking. These are all excellent aerobic exercises, but as you will soon discover, certain calisthenic exercises can be every bit as aerobic and challenging as those already mentioned.

For instance, try doing 500 "Furey Squats" in 20 minutes or less. Notice I said *try*, because they are unbelievably tough. But I'll tell you this, if you *can* do that many, you are obviously in superb shape and have just completed one of the world's best cardio, strength, and flexibility exercises—bar none. In fact, I personally believe the Furey Push-up and the Furey Squat are the two most important and result producing exercises in the entire realm of physical culture.

So there you have it. *Transformetrics*™ *Training System* is made up entirely of the types of exercises just mentioned that have been carefully integrated into one comprehensive health, strength, and body building system. With that said, it's time for Lesson One.

TRANSFORMETRICS

Deep Breathing

PUSHING *to* **POWER**

Super Joints

LESSON ONE

SECTION I: Deep Breathing and Pure Air

SECTION II: Super Joints & Pain-Free Mobility

SECTION III: Chest & Pectoral Exercises

Complete Chest Development

LESSON ONE

"Whatever you can do or dream you can, begin it. Boldness has genius, power, and magic in it. Begin it now."

—GOETHE

Without a doubt, Lesson One is the most important and essential lesson in the entire *Transformetrics™ Training System*. It lays the foundation upon which everything else is built, so please pay special attention to it. I do the Lesson One exercises every morning before work.

Lesson One is divided into three distinct sections.

Section I focuses on the importance of deep breathing, which is the single greatest health builder known to man. Deep breathing should be practiced daily now and throughout your life.

Section II teaches you a system of exercises that require just a few minutes each morning and allows you to move every joint through its *natural* full range of motion. While other authors recommend long static stretches before beginning a workout, and some even advise hyperextension, *this is wrong!* In the morning before your workout, it is important to move all of your joints—in your neck, limbs, torso—extremely *gently* through their *natural* full range of motion. It is likely that your range of motion is impaired through disuse, so don't push it. It will naturally increase as a result of the gentle, consistent practice of the joint mobility exercises found in this section.

Section III. Both *Section I* and *Section II* are to be practiced daily by everyone. However, before moving to *Section III*, you need to make an honest self-assessment. If you are very weak and/or obese, you need to skip *Section III* for the time being and move immediately to Lesson Two on Nutrition and then to Lesson Three on Unlimited Energy. Lesson Three has a special exercise program that will develop your muscles and teach you how to exercise them powerfully without putting your joints or muscles at risk of injury. Once you have either lost the desired amount of body fat or substantially increased your overall strength, it will be perfectly fine to go back to the foundational exercises found in *Section III* of Lesson One.

Section III is a special series of 12 *Transformetric™* exercises and 3 power calisthenic exercises that not only build outstanding strength and shapeliness but also maximize all 7 attributes of true athletic fitness with a special emphasis on chest development.

I do the exercises in *Section I*, *II*, and *III* each morning before I go to work. I do the exercises for the other body parts, which you'll find in Lessons 4 through 12, in 5 to 10 minute intervals throughout the day.

The very first essential step in securing radiant health, strength, and youthfulness is the deep breathing of pure outside air. If you look back through history at the most successful courses on physical culture ever written, *all* of them—not *some* but *all*—focused on this one component. Atlas, Liederman, Farmer Burns, Maxick, George Jowett, Bernan McFadden, Paul Bragg, and so many others made deep breathing their one primary vitality building method of exercise because they understood its true value and did not take it for granted. And why do you suppose they *all* focused so heavily on it? There are many reasons, but here's the foremost reason.

All these men lived at a time when tuberculosis and other respiratory illnesses ravaged the American population. In 1900 the life expectancy was only 48 years for the average American male. Many of them, such as Paul Bragg, who at sixteen was given up as a "hopeless case" of tuberculosis, were restored to health when taken to wilderness retreats as a last resort (no pun intended). They were restored to health as a result of deep breathing of pure outside air, sunshine, vigorous exercise, and natural, health building food with pure water.

In fact, a study of the foundations of physical culture shows that all these men had some form of major disability, and after overcoming it, they decided to dedicate their lives to helping those who were less fortunate and still suffering. Martin "Farmer" Burns, for example, had a course in wrestling and physical culture that was published in the 1910s that was light years ahead of the medical establishment of his time. (This incredible course is available to this day through Matt Furey Enterprises.) This is what Farmer Burns said about the importance of deep breathing and which Matt Furey quotes in many of his books, newsletters, cassettes, and videos. "*Deep breathing alone* has made many a sick man well, and many a weak man strong." Considering that Farmer Burns was the preeminent teacher of catch wrestling in his day, just as Matt Furey is today, and that he was the personal trainer of several world champion wrestlers back at a time when wrestling was *real*, I personally take what he says very seriously.

Your Diaphragm: The Key to Deep Breathing

How do you draw air into the very base of your lungs? Certainly not by merely sniffing it through your nose or by gasping at it with a yawn through your mouth. The natural method of deep breathing—the way babies breathe—is by using the diaphragm to create suction that pulls the air into the lungs. Air may enter the body through either the nose or the mouth, but the force that draws it to fill the air sacs of the lungs to capacity is the muscular action of the diaphragm.

The diaphragm is a dome-shaped sheet of strong muscle fibers that separates the thoracic (upper) half of your body that contains the heart and lungs from the abdominal (lower) cavity that houses the organs of digestion and elimination. It stretches from the sternum in the front across the bottom of the ribs to the spine or backbone.

When the diaphragm expands and flattens moving downward, it produces suction with the chest cavity which causes the inflow of air into the lungs (inhalation). When the diaphragm relaxes and rises, air is forced out of the lungs (exhalation). Both operations are of equal importance . . . inhalation to bring in life-giving oxygen . . . exhalation to expel every bit of poisonous carbon dioxide.

HERE'S WHAT YOU DO.

1. In the morning, while still in bed before arising, consciously relax with your hands at your sides.

2. Inhale deeply through your nose (if you can) and fill your entire body with life-giving oxygen. Imagine your body as one big lung, and as you watch your abdomen rise (just like a baby's), feel the inhale all the way to your feet and let yourself expand.

3. Once you have expanded to the point that you can expand no farther, hold for a slow count of seven seconds, and then begin to slowly exhale.

4. During the exhale, squeeze your abdominals from the top down to the bottom. Squeeze extra hard (great for the abs).

5. As you squeeze, make an "ssss" sound like air being let out of a tire. Continue making this sound until you have forcefully completed your exhale. Endeavor to leave no air in the lungs. Get it all out.

6. Now, start the inhale process all over again, visualizing your body as a giant lung that you will expand as fully as possible. Feel your abdomen rise. Remember, you are breathing naturally like a baby.

7. Practice this deep breathing exercise 10 times every morning before getting out of bed. When you do, you will be amazed at your energy level. If you want, and the weather permits, practice 10 more while standing erect in front of an open window. You'll be amazed at how exhilarating it feels.

I also recommend you do this exercise at several intervals throughout the day, especially when you want to energize and recharge your thought processes or to get rid of mental or emotional stress.

Now that you've read this, let's take action so you can see the value of this incredible health and vitality building exercise. Put the book down, stand up, and complete 10 complete inhalations and exhalations. While you're doing it, remember you are receiving these benefits:

- increased energy and vitality
- increased mental alertness and clarity due to increased oxygen to the brain
- enhanced mental and creative power
- strengthened abdominal muscles
- improved digestion and elimination
- purified lungs (free of stale residue)
- enhanced relaxation
- enhanced power throughout the entire body due to increased oxygenation of the tissues
- improved sexual function (no kidding here)

You can repeat this powerful technique any time you need to recharge your energy and erase the cobwebs from your thinking process. Practice it often.

TRANSFORMETRICS ™ SECTION II
SPECIAL EXERCISES FOR SUPER JOINTS AND LIFELONG PAIN-FREE MOBILITY

These are of vital importance—DO NOT SKIP!

Throughout my years of study in all facets of the martial arts and physical culture, I have known many men and women who have been sidelined, sometimes to the point of being unable to exercise, due to severe injury of the joints and connective tissues of the body. And as a result, some of them have been relegated to a life of pain and a long, slow decline.

This has especially been true of men who exercised exclusively for muscle size and strength by lifting extremely heavy weights. Some of these men were in so much pain that they practically lived on aspirin and other pain medications (how's that for treating a symptom?). Unbeknownst to them, they literally destroyed their joints by exercising to extremes from one angle or direction while neglecting all others. This type of exercise puts excess stress on only one area of the joint, surrounding muscles, and connective tissues, thus creating a tremendous imbalance. Over time, the wear and tear becomes obvious. Some of these geniuses have told me they could actually hear a grating sound while they were lifting.

This abuse is seen in the preoccupation some men have with the Bench Press exercise. Several of the injured men I've know have literally torn their rotator cuff (muscles used in shoulder joint articulation) by overdoing this one exercise. Tell me, how strong is any man when his joints are ruined and he can't even lift his arms, bend his knees, or turn his head without pain?

This is why joint mobility exercises are vitally important. By taking a few minutes to do them daily, they restore your range of motion to what it was in your youth. They also offer immediate feedback by letting you know exactly where the weak, sore, or stiff spots are throughout your body. If you feel pain or impingement while doing any of these exercises, it means you have a problem and need to take immediate action to correct it, before it is too late and causes lifelong injury. If you feel pain, you may want to visit a chiropractor or sports doctor who specializes in working with athletes.

In addition to offering immediate feedback, well lubricated pain-free joints allow you to enjoy life to the fullest and dramatically lessen your susceptibility to injury if you have to move suddenly or if you participate in an activity that is not part of your standard daily routine.

So let's get to them. They're simple to do and require just a few minutes before your workout. They can also be done whenever you want to stretch and de-stress during your day. All that is necessary is just 7 repetitions of each movement. Once you've been doing them for a few weeks, you will always want to do them because, as many of my friends have said, "They feel really good to do."

Study the photos on the following pages closely and do them slowly and as smoothly as possible.

EXERCISE 1
THREE PLAN NECK MOVEMENT

  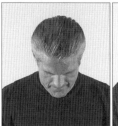   

Look right	Look left	Forward	Backward	Side to side

EXERCISE 2
NECK CIRCLES

7 slow circles in each direction.

EXERCISE 3
SHOULDER ROLLS

Raise shoulders up (toward ears), back, and around. 7 slow reps. Then up, forward, and around.

EXERCISE 4
ARM CIRCLES

7 reps up, back, and around, then 7 reps up, forward, and around.

EXERCISE 5
ELBOW ROTATION

Begin in "up" position, hand follows a half-circle path down and half-circle back to up position. 7 reps each arm.

EXERCISE 6
THE EGYPTIAN

Note: Both palms face "up" as you twist and pivot from side to side.

EXERCISE 7
WRIST ROTATION

Rotate wrist slowly in both directions. 7 reps each way.

EXERCISE 8
HANDS AND FINGERS

Stretch and strengthen fingers and wrists by applying heavy tension and then relaxing.

EXERCISE 9
TORSO TWIST

EXERCISE 10
TORSO ROTATION

EXERCISE 11
BEND, STRETCH, AND TOUCH

Stand 18" to 24" from a wall. Bend backward
slowly touch wall behind you, then bend forward
and try and touch the floor. Just 7 reps is all
that is neccessary.

EXERCISE 12
HIP ROTATION

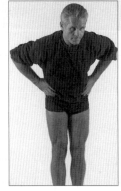   

This is a circular motion.
7 reps each direction.

EXERCISE 13
HALF KNEE BEND

Bend down slowly, but only halfway.

EXERCISE 14
KNEE ROTATION

Bend forward and slowly rotate your knees in a circular movement both to the left and right. (range of motion is limited, so don't push it to far)

EXERCISE 15
ANKLE ROTATION

Rotate each ankle in each direction in small semi-circular movement. 7 reps and switch legs.

EXERCISE 16
TOE RAISE

Slowly raise up and down on toes.
Just 7 reps is all that is neccessary.

The preceding exercises will stretch all the major muscle groups and lubricate all the major joints of the body. Once again, do them slowly and smoothly. If you experience pain, stop immediately. Take note of it and write down specifically where you experienced the pain. This you will want to share with your physician or chiropractor, so he or she can help you rehabilitate that area and prevent further injury. Above all, please be encouraged that many people have been restored to complete pain-free mobility through these exercises. Be patient and persevere. It's only too late if you don't start now.

At this point, before we go further, I want to share with you one important observation. Any exercise system that purports to create good health and true high level physical fitness should always be a safeguard against debilitating pain and injury. Never should it be the cause of it.

"All men and women are born, live, suffer and die; what distinguishes us one from another is our dreams, whether they be dreams about worldly or unworldly things, and what we do to make them come about... We do not choose to be born. We do not choose our parents. We do not choose our historical epoch, the country of our birth, or the immediate circumstances of our upbringing. We do not, most of us, choose to die; nor do we choose the time and conditions of our death. But within this realm of choice-lessness, we do choose how we live."

— JOSEPH EPSTEIN

TRANSFORMETRICS™ SECTION III
FOUNDATIONAL EXERCISES FOR TOTAL STRENGTH AND DEVELOPMENT WITH SPECIAL EMPHASIS ON THE CHEST AND PECTORAL MUSCLES

"If one advances confidently in the direction of his dreams, and endeavors to live the life which he has imagined, he will meet with success unexpected in common hours. He will put some things behind, will pass an invisible boundary; new, universal, and more liberal laws will begin to establish themselves around and within him; or old laws will be expanded and interpreted in his favor in a more liberal sense, and he will live with a license of a higher order of beings."

—Henry David Thoreau

Earle E. Liederman—1919, age 33

John E. Peterson—2003, age 51

CHEST

can still remember as a kid looking at *his* picture on the back of a comic book. First, there was that big smile. *He* looked happy. And then there were those broad shoulders and that powerfully developed chest, tapering to a slim muscular waist. The headline said that even he knew what it was like to get kicked around. At the top of the ad was the little story of "Mac" getting sand kicked in his face, and the invitation to write *him* all seemed so believable. Then you looked back at *him* and thought, *Nobody in their right mind would kick sand in that handsome face . . . not unless they had some strange death wish.*

And, of course, you were right. And so were the hundreds of thousands of other guys who wrote to *him*. And similar to anyone else who followed *his* program faithfully, I got the chest, arms, and shoulders that *he* promised.

Looking back on it, I feel sorry for today's kids who look at the freakish development so prevalent in current muscle magazines without ever seeing *him* for inspiration. How can any kid today even remotely think that what they are seeing in those magazines is believable. Well, the truth is, they can't. But then again, that's good for me because everything I'm about to show you will help anyone, young or old, to develop their chest, arms, and shoulders to their *natural*, God-given best.

Development of the chest was the first priority of both Earle Liederman and Charles Atlas (*him*). The reason is simple: It's not possible to develop your chest without simultaneously developing your arms, shoulders, and upper back. And though both men correctly emphasized the push-up as the key to upper body strength and development, I have a dozen superb DSR and DVR exercises that do the job beautifully. If you decide to use them in conjunction with my high volume push-up program, "How to Go From Zero to 500 Push-ups in 6 Weeks or Less—Guaranteed!" you're going to need to buy new T-shirts because the old ones will be too tight. Let me prove it to you!

Let's get to the exercises.

Please Note:

(DSR) means Dynamic Self-Resistance, where we actually put one set of muscles against another.

(DVR) refers to Dynamic Visualized Resistance, in which your imagination creates the tension in your muscles.

CH-1 (DSR)
LIEDERMAN CHEST PRESS

The following is a word for word description written by Earle E. Liederman. "Clasp hands, or else grip them together as shown in photo #14. Keep them level with chest, then push one hand with the other back and forth across your chest just as far as you can each time. The harder you resist in this exercise, the more benefit you will get out of it. This exercise will outline your pectoral muscles better than any other movement, as it hits them direct."

CH-2 (DVR)
FULL RANGE PECTORAL CONTRACT

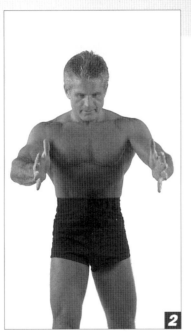

Stand with your left foot in front of your right foot and knee bent back straight (approximately one step, see photo). Hold hands in front, palms facing each other. Bring your hands back slowly with great tension until you feel your back muscles fully flexed. Hold for a count of one thousand one. Then move the hands slowly back to the original position while using great tension in your arms, shoulders, and pectoral muscles. Yes, the muscles will quiver.

CH-3 (DVR)
CROSSOVER PRESS DOWN

First, empty your lungs by crossing your arms in front of your chest and exhaling (see photo #1). Then raise your arms in a circular arc as though you are trying to reach the ceiling at both sides of the room while deeply inhaling. Slowly cross your arms in front with your right hand reaching left and your left hand reaching right. Powerfully contract the pectoral muscles as you try two or three times to reach farther while you exhale. Now raise your arms in a circular arc while inhaling.

This is both a powerful deep breathing and muscle contracting DVR exercise. It is a superb exercise to do anytime throughout the day to revitalize not only your musculature but also your brain with a fresh supply of oxygen. Do it often.

CH-4 (DVR)
ROPE PULL DOWN

Begin with your hands placed around an imaginary rope just above head level (see photo #1). Left hand over right, start pulling down with your left hand against the strong resistance of your right hand. Make it hard and pull the full range of movement as shown. The key is the powerful contraction of the pectorals caused by the top and bottom hands resisting each other. Switch hands to right over left. Continue 3 to 5 times with each hand in the top position.

CH-5 (DSR)

Place your left fist in the palm of your right hand on a level with the hips (see photo). Both hands are over your right hip with elbows bent. Against the powerful resistance of your right hand, endeavor to push your left hand down to the right side until your left elbow is no longer bent. This exercise is great for the pecs, arms, and shoulders.

CH-6 (DSR)
PULL APART, UP AND OVER

Grip the middle fingers of each hand as shown. Pull outward powerfully while raising your arms up, over, and back of your head. Maintain tension and reverse the direction of the arms until you reach the starting position. Continue 3 to 5 reps at extra heavy tension.

CH-7 (DSR)
LIEDERMAN PECTORAL CONTRACTION

Initially, this may seem like an odd exercise, but wait till you try it. It is odd, but effective! Squat down as shown in the photo, heels approximately six inches apart and knees spread wide. Place your hands on the outside of your knees and endeavor to push your knees together against the powerful resistance of your knees pushing outward. Your pecs and arms get an incredible workout.

CH-8 (DSR)
C'MON AT YA!

With your hands in a prayer posture at the center of your chest (see photo #1) and with both hands applying extra heavy resistance, slowly extend your arms. After achieving full extension, return to the start position while maintaining the tension. Each repetition will require 10-12 seconds to complete. 3-5 reps max, while maintaining extra-heavy tension.

CH-9 (DSR)

Assume the position shown in photo #1 with both your hands pressing powerfully toward each other. While maintaining this intense pressure with your arms bent, simultaneously inhale and slowly raise your hands to the position in photo #3. At the top of the movement, relax all your muscles momentarily while exhaling powerfully. Then regain the inward pressure of your hand and slowly lower to the starting position. Repeat the entire process 2 to 4 additional repetitions.

CH-10 (DVR)
(NOT PICTURED)

While standing erect, hands at sides, bear down on your shoulders and arms at the same time and consciously contract the pectoral muscles. This exercise is excellent for muscle control and can be practiced whenever you think of it throughout the day.

CH-11 (DSR)
(NOT PICTURED)

Stand with the palm of each hand pressing upon the top of your thighs. Your arms and legs are straight with all your muscles tightly contracted. Lean forward with great tension as your arms contract powerfully against your thighs and allow your hands to slide until they reach the knees. You'll notice that your abs as well as your pectorals and triceps can achieve peak contraction.

CH-12 (DSR)
PECTORAL PUSH DOWN WHILE SEATED

While sitting in a chair, grasp the seat with both hands and raise your body slightly with your legs extended. Raise up and down several times.
An advanced variation is to do this exercise while holding on to the armrests of a chair. (see photo)

One More Thought...

In addition to the first 12 exercises presented so far, I encourage you to perform what I believe to be the three most important power calisthenic exercises in the entire realm of physical culture. They teach the muscles of the entire body to work together in unison and can dramatically enhance your speed, flexibility, balance, coordination, and endurance, in addition to the strength and aesthetics that are already achieved through performance of the first series of 12 exercises. These exercises in order of importance are in the next three pages to come:

1. The Furey Push-up

2. The Furey Squat

3. The Atlas Push-up

THE FUREY PUSH-UP

In February 2000, Matt Furey published his groundbreaking bestseller, *Combat Conditioning*. As a result, athletes and physical culturists the world over were introduced to a revolutionary exercise system that not only enhanced every attribute of dynamic strength and athletic fitness but also helped thousands to rehabilitate and rebuild their bodies to a point previously unimagined. I know. I was personally among them.

One of the key exercises Matt teaches is the Furey Push-up. In his book, he calls it the Hindu Push-up, but I call it the Furey Push-up because if it were not for Matt Furey the entire Western world would be unaware of this incredible exercise. This is how it is done.

Photo #1. Start with your hands on the floor, shoulder-width apart, and your head tucked in and looking directly at your feet. Your feet are shoulder-width apart or slightly wider. Your legs and back are straight, and your butt is the highest point of the body.

Photos #2-3-4-5. Bend your elbows while descending in a smooth circular arc almost brushing your chest and upper body to the floor as you continue the circular range of motion until your arms are straight, back flexed, and hips almost, but not quite, touching the floor.

Photo #6. At the top of the movement, look at the ceiling while consciously flexing your triceps and exhaling.

Photo #7. Raise your hips and buttocks while simultaneously pushing back with straight arms, causing a complete articulation of both shoulder joints.

Photo #8. Arrive at the starting position with your legs and back straight, your head tucked in, and eyes looking at your feet.

Continue as smoothly and as fluidly as possible for as many repetitions as you can do.

At the beginning, anywhere from 15 to 25 repetitions is excellent. I know guys who can bench press 400 pounds who couldn't do 25 in a row if you had a gun to their head. Once you can routinely do sets of 50 or more, you will have superb shoulder, chest, arm, and both upper and lower back development.

In my opinion this is the single greatest exercise known to man because it exercises every muscle from your neck to your toes and on both front and back sides of the body. Repetition for repetition it delivers the highest level of strength, flexibility, and endurance of any calisthenic exercise known. In fact, it is the one exercise that comes closest to duplicating the exact movement of large jungle cats. It is truly one magnificent exercise.

THE FUREY SQUAT

This is definitely not your garden-variety knee bend. I consider it a close runner-up to the Furey Push-up in its order of calisthenic importance, only because it doesn't have quite the same overall bodybuilding effect. But it's close. When done in very high repetitions, I believe it is the world's preeminent cardiovascular exercise. Here is how it's done.

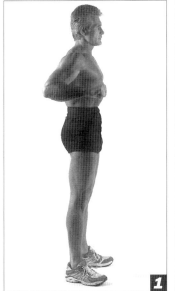

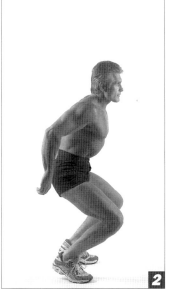

Photo #1. Feet approximately shoulder-width apart. Toes straight ahead. Hands in tight fists at shoulder level. Inhale deeply.

Photo #2. While keeping your back relatively straight (don't bend forward), bend your knees and descend to the bottom position.

Photo #3. Note the position of the hands reaching behind your back during the descent and brushing your knuckles on the ground at the bottom (how's that for a knuckle dragger?).

Photo #4. When you arrive at the bottom position, you will rise naturally to your toes. This is superb for your balance.

Photo #5. At this point your arms continue swinging forward and upward while simultaneously pushing off your toes and rising to the original standing position.

Photo #6. Your hands now form tight fists close to your sides at chest level. Inhale as you pull them in, exhale as you lower your body.

Repeat as smoothly and steadily as you can. Once you begin you'll notice that the arms take on a smooth, rhythmic motion similar to rowing a boat.

The entire movement of steps 1 to 6 is one continuous, smooth movement. 25 to 50 repetitions is a great start. 100 without stopping is excellent. Once you can do 500 in 20 minutes or less, you have accomplished the world's preeminent cardiovascular workout, not to mention a superb upper and lower leg workout.

FOR THE TRULY HARDCORE

For men and women who are already in phenomenal shape, try the one-legged squat which is shown to the left.

If you can do 10 with either leg, you're *a man*—even if you happen to be a woman, *you're a man.*

THE ATLAS PUSH-UP

In his world-famous bodybuilding course first published in 1922, Charles Atlas prominently featured only one type of push-up. It was the very first exercise of his entire system of training. And he made no bones about it. In his opinion this was the preeminent exercise for strength conditioning and physical development. Up until I came across the Furey Push-up and Squat, I agreed with Mr. Atlas. It is a superb exercise, but now I place it at number 3. I do all three exercises both morning and evening.

With two chairs side by side (between 18" and 26" apart, depending upon your shoulder width and arm length), place a hand on the seat of each chair (photo #1). Your body is extended in a sloping position with your feet on the floor. Now perform a push-up between the chairs, allowing your chest to descend as close to the floor as is comfortable (photo #2). Do not force yourself to descend beyond what is comfortable. In time your range of motion will naturally increase. Smoothly extend your arms to complete extension for one complete repetition.

Do as many as you can and as smoothly as possible. This is a superb deep breathing and pectoral development exercise. Atlas recommended that a total of 200 be performed if you want superb chest development. It is also a great exercise for the triceps of the upper arm and the latissimus dorsi muscles of the upper back. If you can perform sets of 25 or more, you are doing great.

VARIATION

This exercise is performed exactly as above except that your feet are now elevated to a level equal to or higher than the hands. This variation changes the emphasis of development from the lower pectoral line to more of the middle pectoral muscles. If your feet are raised higher than the hands, the emphasis is changed to upper pectorals and deltoids. (please note: your abs get a great workout by maintaining flawless form as shown.)

The most extreme version of the Atlas push-up is one I learned from Matt Furey. It is the Furey Extended Range Handstand Push-up between chairs (see photos below). It is singularly the most difficult and result-producing upper body push-up known, requiring incredible strength to perform even once. I'm of the opinion that less than 3 percent of the world's strongest athletes would be capable of doing it for repetitions.

GOD CREATED *YOU* TO BE AN ORIGINAL

Well, there you have Lesson One in its entirety. Practice it exclusively for the next 3 to 4 weeks. During this time I encourage you to also practice the nutritional advice found in Lesson Two and to pay special attention to the Energy and Self-Improvement advice in Lesson Three.

Although I have given you a wide range of incredible exercises that produce great results, don't be afraid to experiment with your own tempo, your own prescription of sets and repetitions, or the intensity that is right for you. Always keep in mind that once you master the fundamental concepts, it is time to rely on yourself and your own intuition to create the best possible program for you.

Never forget that God created *You* to be an original, not a cheap copy of someone else.

Question & Answer

Q: Is running the best way to lose body fat?

A: Best? Go watch a marathon sometime and tell me what you see. You'll see alot of scrawny looking guys with weak upper bodies and loose fat on their abdomens and lower back (love handles). I'm not saying running isn't a good endurance builder—it is. I'm just saying that it isn't an efficient fat burner because it accelerates muscle loss in the upper body. And if you continually lose muscle mass you will start to *gain fat*! From my perspective, the best cardio routine on the planet to help you lose body fat is one that combines Furey Push-ups with Furey Squats. This is because you simultaneously build muscle mass while enhancing strength, flexibility, balance, coordination, endurance, speed, and aesthetics. Once you can do 3 to 5 sets of 30-50 Furey Push-ups and can complete 500 Furey Squats in 20 minutes or less you will have discovered the ultimate fat-burning routine.

NUTRITION

Dieting

Calories

LESSON TWO

PUSHING YOURSELF to POWER

FAT

"I am convinced that a light supper, a good night's sleep, and a fine morning, have sometimes made a hero of the same man who, by an indigestion, a restless night, and rainy morning, would have proved a coward."

—Lord Chesterfield

LESSON TWO

To create the body of a warrior/athlete, you need the right building materials in the right portions. I will now share with you the right way to feed your body for maximum strength, athletic fitness, and total rejuvenation. But before I do, I want to clarify that this is *not* going to be a senseless, self-serving, self-righteous diatribe to make you feel guilty.

What do I mean by that? Well, it's like this. Years ago one of my karate buddies (Wayne) came across a newspaper article that said a world famous swimming coach who had recently swum the English Channel was giving a evening lecture at the University of Minnesota campus. The topic: "Fitness and Nutrition for Maximum Athletic Performance." Price: $10 a head, which back in 1976 was about the equivalent of $30 in 2003.

Wayne and I arrived early to get the best seats in the middle of the front row of the packed auditorium. Finally, someone introduced the speaker Coach Jim (I don't want to be sued). I'll never forget it as long as I live. When this guy came out, he was a grossly overweight, misshapen hulk of a man with loose hanging fat, spindly arms, and a gut that looked as though he must have been training in the pubs of Ireland on gallons of Guinness Extra Stout every day for six months prior to the swim. Wayne turned to me and said, "I can't believe we spent ten bucks apiece to hear *him*. He didn't swim anywhere. He just floated across on the tide like a bar of soap."

It was hard to dispute the point. And when this guy tried telling us how to feed an athlete's body, it became downright laughable. Listening to him was like listening to a derelict bum on skid row tell you how to become a millionaire in five easy steps. It just wasn't believable. And besides, everything he said to avoid at all costs, such as red meat and all dairy products, made no sense coming from a man who looked like the twin brother of Jabba the Hutt of *Star Wars*. (Okay, I have to stop here. My mom's going to read this.) Wayne and I got up to leave, and we weren't the only ones leaving.

Bottom line: No one should ever tell anyone else how to live, pray, train, or eat unless he or she is an example.

So what is the best way to feed yourself for health, strength, and rejuvenation? Once again, I refer back to Charles Atlas. In his classic course written back in the early 1920s, Mr. Atlas made a point of telling his students to eat well and eat often. His emphasis was on fresh vegetables, fresh fruits, lean meats, and whole-grain breads and cereals. His whole approach was based on *what to* eat, *not* what to avoid. He even told you that while candy should not be a dominant part of your diet, it should be of the highest possible quality when you do indulge. Now that's my kind of advice. In fact, the only dietary advice that Mr. Atlas gave that I would even question today is his strong recommendation to consume large quantities of whole milk in order to gain muscle size. While this worked well for some of my underweight buddies in junior high, today there are some incredible weight-gain formulas readily available in health food stores that accomplish the goal more quickly without all the fat of whole milk. However, given a choice between whole milk and the soda pop so readily available in American schools, Charles Atlas was right. Milk is a far better choice.

That said, let's take a look at eating for health, strength, and rejuvenation. And while we're at it, let's zero in on how to get "ripped to the bone," since most people want that look.

The word "diet" has gotten such a bad reputation that I hesitate to use it. (Maybe that's because the word "die" is in it?) But *what you eat is your diet*. In fact, *Webster's* defines "diet" this way: "1) food and drink regularly provided or consumed; habitual nourishment."

Some people, such as the world famous coach, "regularly consume" high-fat, high-sugar, low-nutrient foods. While others eat low-fat, low-sugar, high-nutritional foods. *Both are on a specific diet*. And it shows! With this in mind, I hope you will rethink the word "diet" and cut me a little slack for using it from time to time.

In this lesson, you'll find out how to make sure that your diet includes nutritious, low-fat foods that will ultimately result in the loss of any excess fat that may be lingering on your body. If you follow the simple food formula presented here, in time you will be able to stand in front of a mirror after a shower and honestly say, "I like what I see." At that point you will be given a plan to maintain your sculpted body—a system so simple that at first you'll think it can't possibly be true. But it is!

First the facts.

Why People Get Fat

If this subhead seems like a "duh" to you, bear with me or skip to the next point. It's a point that must be made for those who just don't understand.

All food contains potential energy, which is defined as "calories." When we eat food, either we use the food and burn it up as energy, or it gets stored on our body as fat. If we keep eating more food than we burn, we get fat. In fact, we can become obese.

Perhaps you have a grand storehouse of fat. Perhaps a hundred pounds of fat. How do you get rid of it? Slowly and calmly.

You will now follow a fool-proof plan that forces your body to use up stored fat day by day while nourishing you to the max. In time, the entire storehouse will be depleted, and the tight, lithe muscles you have been developing with this training system will be perfectly displayed. You'll love your body.

Making It Happen

But how can you make this happen? You've already taken the first fat-burning step without even having begun a low-fat diet. How so? By having begun the workouts, which ultimately puts sculpted, shapely muscles all over your body and causes you to burn fat twenty-four hours a day, seven days a week. In fact, I've got three essential figures that you should remember and imbed in your consciousness (in other words, memorize them).

3,500—number of calories stored in one pound of fat.

35—number of calories burned by one pound of muscle each day.

2—number of calories burned by one pound of fat each day.

Armed with this information, it's easy to understand that if you were at caloric equilibrium (neither gaining nor losing weight), and you add 10 pounds of muscle through *Transformetrics*™, your body will naturally burn off 1 pound of body fat every 10 days (350 X 10 = 3,500). But by simultaneously building muscle and restricting caloric intake, you can easily lose 1 pound of fat every 5 days. In 90 days that equals 18 pounds of body fat. Now, if you were to lose 18 pounds of fat over the next 3 months and replace it with 18 pounds of lean muscle, don't you think it would create a startling change in your appearance and fitness level, even if the scale showed zero change in your body weight?

Food Facts

Nutritional science divides food into three groups: fats, proteins, and carbohydrates. In order to lose maximum body fat while maintaining maximum nutrition, your daily intake *should* consist of approximately 15 percent fat, 15 percent protein, and 70 percent unrefined carbohydrates. But why in those percentages?

Perhaps a personal story will help answer that. Back in 1981, I was fanatical about long distance running and had run several marathons. For whatever reason, I decided I was to going to run an upcoming October marathon in 2 hours, 36 minutes or less, thereby averaging 6 minutes per mile for the entire 26 miles and 385 yards.

To accomplish this, I determined to do two things. First, I'd up my daily mileage to 12, or 84 miles a week. This was in addition to my strength training. Next, I was going to intentionally drop 10 pounds of body weight, which at that time was 170 pounds as a result of my intense running. (My best standard body weight is 178-182 pounds.) It was important to me to maintain a beautifully sculpted, lithe, ultra-hard, athletic body, so I decided to follow the dieting information found in bodybuilder Clarence Bass's classic

book on diet and training, *Ripped*. In it, he shared the exact strategies he used to get his body fat down to 2.4 percent. I followed his diet recommendations to the letter, which are virtually identical to what I will share with you (except that Clarence recommended going almost completely vegetarian).

The diet worked like a dream. In fact, when October came, I didn't weigh 160, I weighed all of 152 pounds. I literally looked as though someone had stretched my skin over raw muscles and bones. I was precisely at 3.2 percent body fat, and I was so overtrained it was ridiculous. Plus I was edgy all the time. Not the kind of guy you'd want to hang out with. And if I stood up too fast, I'd almost black out because my blood pressure had gotten so low. In addition, once I was below 155 pounds my strength training started getting much harder, although I had set a personal record for pull-ups with a set of 54 continuous, flawless reps when I weighed 158 pounds.

On marathon day, I ran my dead level best. You could have put a gun to my head and I could not have run any faster. And my time, after all that work and dieting, was 2 hours, 43 minutes, and 37 seconds. I was miserable, and my nerves were fried. I felt weak and emaciated. And as I was resting after the race, one of the front runners, a wispy, thin guy who owned the store where I bought my running shoes, came over to congratulate me. He said to me, "You know, if you'd lose 15 to 20 pounds, you'd be at the front of the pack." In retrospect, I know he was trying to be nice and complimentary. But I didn't take it that way then. I was too weak to punch him, so instead I was very rude. What I said to him I can't repeat here, but I can tell you I did go to his store the next weekend to apologize.

I tell this story because I want you to know that this diet works perfectly, and if I had not been running to such an extreme level, I would not have gotten so weak. Bottom line: 15 percent fat, 15 percent protein, and 70 percent carbohydrates, most of which were unrefined, worked beautifully. The secret is to eat no food that has high concentrations of fat and sugar. That automatically means no ice cream, pies, cookies, cakes, or candies. No pastries and no booze. (I know that booze doesn't have any fat, but alcohol has an effect like sugar, and it also slows your metabolic rate.)

Once you've reached a point where you are as fat free as you want to be, you will slowly add both protein and fat to your diet and rely less on carbohydrates, or you will continue to lose weight. In fact, my diet is currently comprised of 20-30 percent fat, 30 percent protein, and 40-50 percent carbohydrates. Following this diet, I stay right at 178-182 pounds with no effort. If I want to go for ultra-high definition, I just revert back to 15/15/70, and within a month I'm ultra-ripped.

So now that you know the *why* of the percentages of fat, protein, and carbohydrates, let's look at each of them separately.

Fat

In simple terms, eating fat makes you fat. Why? Because it has more than twice the number of calories per gram (9 calories per fat gram) than carbohydrates (4 calories per gram). In addition, when fat is digested, very little energy is expended, whereas proteins and carbohydrates burn up about 20 percent of their calories in the digestive process alone.

Where is fat found? Virtually everywhere! It's even found in the most healthful foods—in mod-

est amounts. For example, an average size apple has 1 gram of fat. You will consume most of your fat allotment in your protein requirement. The rest will be spread out—a gram here, a gram there, until you reach your full allotment.

Protein

Protein is necessary for a balanced diet and to build muscle. Only small amounts can be used productively by the human body at any given time. Overindulgence in protein is stored on the body as fat. Therefore, only 15 percent of your total food volume will be in the form of protein. Protein is found in all meat, poultry, fish, eggs, beans, and dairy products. As you can see, since most protein comes in foods that are high in fat, you have to be careful where you get your protein. You'll be given the best sources of lean protein later in this chapter.

Carbohydrates

Carbohydrates provide you with energy for both your body and your mind. *If you deplete your body of carbohydrates, you're going to suffer.* After a while you'll start to feel weak, and then you'll start to feel edgy and lose control over your emotions. In fact, you won't even be able to think straight. For this reason, 70 percent of your food allotment comes from natural, unrefined carbohydrates.

Carbohydrates fall into two main categories: *simple* and *complex*. *Simple* carbohydrates are divided into two subcategories: good and bad. *Good* simple carbohydrates are found in fruits of all types. *Bad* simple carbohydrates are refined carbohydrates—in other words, all sugars!

To accomplish your goal, it is absolutely necessary to keep your intake of bad simple carbohydrates (sugars) as low as possible. Please note: I'm not saying you can't have any. But keep it low because it can and does hinder fat-burning. Why?

Because when you consume a substantial amount of sugar, a heavy dose of glucose is released into your bloodstream, causing your body to produce high levels of insulin. This, in turn, inhibits hormone-sensitive lipase, the enzyme that is responsible for draining fat from the cells. That's the exact opposite of what you want. When it comes to sugar, keep it to a bare minimum, and if in doubt, leave it out. I know that's easier said than done, but it can be done.

Complex carbohydrates include all vegetables, whole-grain breads and cereals, rice, and pasta. When you are on a regular exercise program, such as *Transformetrics*™, your body will actually crave carbohydrates. On the other hand, as you might have already noticed, if you do no exercise, your body craves fat.

When possible, it's always better to eat whole-grain bread, pasta, or rice as opposed to "white." Why? The white varieties have been processed and refined, transforming them into starches that behave as sugars. I personally have no problem avoiding white pasta and white rice (no, it's not because I think I'm Superman), but I have a lot of friends who seem to crave it. In such cases, I recommend that you cook your white pasta "al dente" (slightly firm), which keeps it from behaving as sugar, according to several leading nutritionists.

How Much of Each Group Should You Eat?

So how do you figure out the percentages? Don't bother with a calculator. I've already done it for you. If you follow the food plan I outline, you will automatically be consuming about 15 percent fat, 15 percent protein, and 70 percent carbohydrates.

> *"Never eat more than you can lift."*
> —Miss Piggy

The only math you'll have to do is addition—and that will be for fat grams exclusively. If you are a man, you will want to keep your daily fat grams between 30-40 grams in order to lose body fat quickly and safely. If you are a woman, your daily fat grams will range between 20-25 grams.

"Don't know her guys, but she sure takes a nice photo."
—J.P.

Naturally, depending upon your size and shape, the lower end is better for faster fat loss. If you want to keep your daily fat intake even lower, you can, but don't go lower than 10 percent of your daily caloric intake. If you do, you will constantly feel hungry and won't know why. Also, virtually everything I have read by competent nutritionists over the last two decades agrees that this is the bare minimum amount for good health. Any less than that and your body won't be able to manufacture hormones. By way of example, this would mean that you would have a minimum of 20 grams of fat in an 1800-calorie diet or 180 calories of fat.

A Balanced Diet

Most health and nutrition experts agree that a daily balanced diet should contain the following:

Bare minimum of fats, sugars, and refined carbohydrates

> 2-3 servings of low-fat dairy products
> 2-3 servings of lean protein
>
> 3-5 servings of vegetables
> 2-4 servings of fruit
>
> 6-12 servings of whole-grain breads, grains, pastas, rice, or cereals

I have taken that guideline and modified it to fit in with this low-fat weight-loss plan. I've adjusted the pyramid so that you can lose the maximum amount of body fat and at the same time ensure optimal health. In the following paragraphs, you will be told which foods are acceptable for the low-fat eating plan, and how much of each of these foods constitutes a serving. In the end, it will be a simple matter for you to make up your own daily meal plan. All you have to do is pick out servings from each group. You need not be bored with same old, same old. You can have something different every day of the month. It's up to you.

Let's take a closer look at each specific food group to determine what constitutes a realistic serving of each particular group in the five distinctive food groups.

You Will Eat 6-11 Servings of Limited Complex Carbohydrates (preferably natural and whole-grain varieties)

Note: In general, depending upon your size, men will eat the amount closer to the maximum number of servings, and women will eat closer to the minimum. However, women who are more than 20 pounds overweight may opt for the maximum amount.

This group of complex carbohydrates provides high energy. It includes whole-grain breads and cereals, rice, pasta, and all grains, plus several high carbohydrate vegetables. (see list one)

List One

One serving is equal to:

> 2 slices of whole wheat bread
> 1/2 bagel
> 1 English muffin
> 3 cups of air-popped popcorn
> 1/2 cup hot cooked cereal
> 3/4 cup dry cold cereal
> 2/3 cup cooked pasta or rice
> 1/3 cup barley
> 1 ounce of pretzels
> 8 low-fat medium crackers
> 4 rice cakes
> 1 medium potato
> 1 small yam or sweet potato
> 1 cup beets or peas
> 1 cup of corn
> 1 large corn on the cob
> 3/4 cup Jerusalem artichoke
> 1 cup acorn squash

Okay, now let's go through an average day and see how much food you really get to eat, looking at the maximum allowance first for men and for women who are 20 pounds or more overweight.

You can have a whole bagel for breakfast (2 servings), 1-1/2 cups of rice with lunch (2 servings), a generous amount of pretzels for a snack (2 servings),

2 cups of pasta for dinner (3 servings), and 2 rice cakes for snack (1/2 serving), and still be within the fat-loss range. In addition, you have all the other foods to eat.

What? Too much food? You can go closer to the minimum if you want, or anywhere in between, and still be within the range of healthful eating.

You Will Eat 6 or More Servings of Vegetables (preferably much more of these complex carbohydrates)

And any vegetable except those already listed on the previous list (corn, potatoes, beets, Jerusalem artichokes, acorn squash, and peas) is fair game. (see list two)

List Two

One serving is equal to (1/2 cup cooked or 1 cup raw):

- Asparagus
- Broccoli
- Brussel sprouts
- Cabbage
- Carrots
- Cauliflower
- Celery
- Chicory
- Collard greens
- Cucumber
- Eggplant
- Endive
- Escarole
- Frozen mixed vegetables
- Green or yellow beans
- Kale
- Leeks
- Lettuce
- Mushrooms
- Okra
- Onions
- Parsnips
- Peppers
- Radishes
- Rutabagas
- Shallots
- Sprouts
- Squash

Time to think this through. You already know what you were allowed to have from List One. Now, in addition to that you can have six or more servings from the above list. That's six or more whole cups of vegetables. Well, how about it?

Could you really eat that much and not feel stuffed? Of course not. That's the whole idea. You can eat as much of and as many of the above vegetables and still lose weight. How so? They are *very* low in calories and at the same time filling. The human stomach is incapable of holding more than 2 pounds of food at one time. You really can't overdo vegetables. And frankly, I've never heard of anyone overdoing it on vegetables.

But did you know that in order to be healthy you *must* consume at least two cups of vegetables a day. Why? Because they are filled with fiber, vitamins, minerals, phyto-nutrients, and other nutrients that not only keep you healthy and looking good, but ward off all kinds of diseases.

So you *must*, I repeat *must*, eat vegetables. No ifs, ands, or buts about it. You will learn to love them and even thank God for creating them. How so? If you limit your food intake to the guidelines in this chapter, you'll be hungry, plain and simple. The combination of *Transformetrics*™ and the intake of the right percentage of foods will push your metabolism to peak performance and burn the calories. In time you'll be glad to have anything legitimate to eat. And what now may seem unthinkable will be a pleasure then.

But do yourself a favor. Don't eat the same vegetables each day. Experiment. Go to the supermarket and buy all kinds of frozen vegetables in family-size bags. Check the label to make sure that no fat is added. Go to the produce counter and purchase a variety of vegetables. Believe it or not, it won't be long before you're looking forward to vegetables instead of dreading them. You'll even be able to cook up a whole family-size bag and eat it all in one sitting! No Guilt. In fact, you'll feel great about it.

You Will Eat 2-4 Servings of Simple Carbohydrates Daily—Fruit

One serving equals:

  1 large piece of any fruit: apple, orange, pear, etc.

  1 cup of berries of any kind

  1 cup of mango or papaya

  1-1/2 cups of strawberries or watermelon

  1/2 cantaloupe, grapefruit, or large plantain

  1/4 honeydew melon or pineapple

  1 large banana

  20 cherries

  20 grapes

  4 persimmons or kumquats

  3 large plums or tangerines

Think of it, you could eat a whole quart of berries, or six cups of strawberries, or an entire pineapple, or any combination of the above, and still lose body fat. In addition, you would be fueling your body with incredibly high amounts of vitamins, minerals, and enzymes that would also help you add muscle mass while getting ultra-lean.

You Will Eat 2-3 Servings of Lean Protein

One serving equals 4-6 ounces of white chicken or turkey or fish. This means that all poultry is cooked without the skin and without fat.

On the following list I show both fat grams and protein grams. Please note: multiply both protein and fat by 1.5 if you use 6-ounce portions as I do. (see list three)

But what about your fat allotment? How will a woman get 20-25 grams or a man 30-40 grams daily? For the most part you will have already consumed it in the foods you've eaten. But if in doubt, get yourself a fat gram counter and count up your daily fat grams. Keep in mind, though, the numbers listed above are only for those times when you are on an intense fat-loss program. Once you have achieved your goal, you could literally eat 30 percent protein, 30 percent fat, and 40 percent carbohydrates and gain no body fat. At that point, it will be up to you to monitor your intake to determine at what point your body does start storing fat.

List Three
Protein/Fat

Poultry (4 ounces cooked)

	Protein Grams	Fat Grams
Turkey Breast	34	1
Turkey Drumstick	33	4.5
Turkey Thigh	31	5
Chicken Breast	35	4.5
Chicken Drumstick	37	6.8
Chicken Thigh	31	5

Fish (4 ounces cooked)

Mahi Mahi	20.8	.8
Haddock	23	1
Cod	26	1
Abalone	16	1
Sole	19	1
Pike	25	1
Scallops	26	1
Tuna in water	34	1
Squid	20	1.8
Flounder	34	2.3
Red Snapper	26	2.3
Sea Bass	25	3.4
Halibut	31	4
Trout	30	4

Vegetarian Sources

3 Egg Whites	9	1
1/2 Cup Beans	9	1
1/2 Cup Soft Tofu	10	6
1/2 Cup Firm Tofu	10	11

You Will Eat 2-3 Dairy Foods Daily

One serving equals	Protein Grams	Fat Grams
8 ounces low-fat yogurt	12	4
8 ounces no-fat yogurt	12	0
8 ounces 1% milk	9	3
8 ounces skim milk	9	0
4 ounces 1% cottage cheese	14	1
2 tablespoons no-fat cream cheese	2	0
2 slices no-fat cheese	12	0
1/2 cup no-fat ice cream	2	0

If you can't consume dairy products due to lactose intolerance, there are some wonderful soy substitutes, but watch your fat grams.

Time to Review

To lose body fat on the hurry up, you do the following.

1. EAT YOUR MINIMUM FOR THE DAY.

- 6 to an unlimited number of servings of vegetables (both raw and cooked)

- 6-11 servings of complex carbohydrates

- 2-4 servings of fruit (fresh, frozen, or canned in juice with no sugar)

- 2-3 servings of lean protein, 4-6 ounces each

- 2-3 servings of dairy or substitute dairy products.

2. EAT OFTEN. 5-6 times a day. Don't go more than 4 hours without eating something.

3. HYDRATE YOURSELF. Drink lots of pure water, 8-12 glasses each day. Charles Atlas recommended a glass of water first thing in the morning with half of a freshly squeezed lemon.

4. ENJOY YOURSELF. If you're at someone's house, don't be a jerk. Go ahead and enjoy yourself once in a while. The key to fat loss is what you do on a consistent basis—not what you do once in a while.

5. DON'T OVERDO IT. Be good to yourself. Listen to your body. Don't force yourself to live on minimums of anything. If you do, you will lose strength, and that's the last thing you want to happen.

6. BE SMART. Once people start complimenting you on the marvelous changes taking place, realize that you're doing everything right. Don't try to accelerate anything by eating too little or working out too often. If you do, you'll defeat your purpose, and in time you'll look like you've spent years in forced prison labor while building the bridge over the River Kwai. Not a good thing.

Well, there you have it. Follow these guidelines and you can get as lean as you want. But remember: once you achieve your goal, it's important to start adding both protein and fat and cutting down somewhat on the carbohydrates or you may lose too much *weight*. By that I mean *muscle weight*.

An Afterthought

Perhaps you're wondering if this Peterson guy's "ripped to the bone" diet recommendations have ever not worked. To be totally honest, there was one time when it didn't—*sort of*. It happened with my friend Greg. Greg's a self-made man. You know the type—off-the-charts intelligence, no formal education, but street smarts that more than compensate for it. Really a sharp, sharp man. This is what happened.

Greg wanted to take his wife, Wendy, for a two-week trip to Jamaica for their tenth anniversary honeymoon celebration. They were going to renew their wedding vows and then just kick back and spend time together diving, snorkeling, and wind surfing. So Greg came to me, wanting to get in shape on the hurry up. No problem. With the guts and determination this guy has, I knew he'd follow all my recommendations to the letter. And sure enough, his chest, arms, shoulders, and back started to fill out his sport coats. He even became a Furey Push-up fanatic, doing 150 of that one variation alone every day.

But about ten weeks into the program I saw him in church, and it was obvious he was put out with me. So during the time of greeting just before the sermon, I went and asked if everything was okay between us. He said that he had been working his "butt off," but with only two weeks before the trip, his abs still weren't showing even though he did all the ab exercises and was now cranking 500 push-ups a day. He was adamant that my dietary recommendations weren't working because, as he said, "The muscles feel like they're made out of steel. You just can't see 'em clearly."

So we got together after church to discuss it, and it was amazing. He had followed everything precisely and even wrote it all down. He admitted that he was in the best shape of his life and never looked better, but the abs were a disappointment. Finally, I said, "Look, Greg, you must be taking in hidden calories somewhere. What are you drinking these days besides water?" He looked me straight in the eye and said, "Well, I usually have a bottle of wine with lunch, and another bottle at dinner, and a few shots of Sauza Tres Generaciones Tequila in between. Why? Are there any calories in those?"

Now you know what I mean by *sort of*.

By the way, the church that my wife and I attend strongly recommends that its parishioners abstain from all alcoholic beverages. We even use grape juice instead of wine for communion. Nonetheless, for the sake of accuracy, I thought I should report the above incident as it actually happened.

Question & Answer

Q: How important is feeling "The Burn"?

A: If you want to feel a burn, hold on to a match or put your hand over a burning candle and then tell me how important it was.

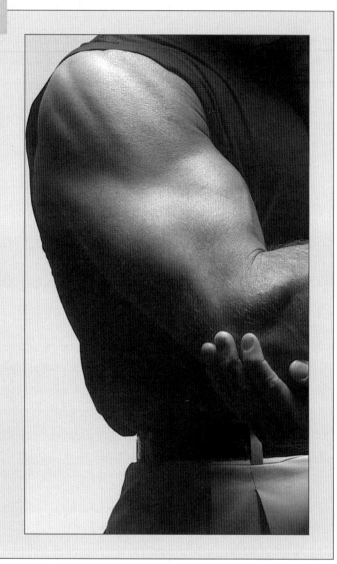

Renew

ENERGY

Revitalize

LESSON THREE
PUSHING YOURSELF
to POWER

Recharge

LESSON THREE

HOW TO RENEW, RECHARGE, AND REVITALIZE YOUR BODY, MIND, AND SPIRIT
(Of Special Importance to the Obese and Weak)

By now you are well on your way to shaping the kind of body you've always dreamed could be yours. You've learned the fundamentals of *Transformetrics*™ *Strength Training* and are aware of over 100 exercises that will develop every muscle in your body without you ever having to go to the gym. You've also learned the fundamentals of proper nutrition and even how to get "ripped," if that's your goal.

Now we're going to tackle a much bigger issue—your energy level—upon which so much of your physical, financial, intellectual, social, and spiritual success depends. Without an abundance of *energy*, you won't be able to follow any exercise program. No, in fact you will feel lethargic and depressed all the time. You won't be able to give your family, your spouse, your friends, or your career the attention they deserve. Most of all, you will be robbing yourself of the joy of living that you *could* have if you had an abundance of—you guessed it—*Energy!*

So let's focus clearly on how to become a "Human Dynamo"—a person who's in love with life and energized 24 hours a day, 7 days a week.

You Are Fearfully and Wonderfully Made

You in your own person—mind (intellect and emotions), body, and spirit—are a marvel of God's creation. In fact, in the Bible, King David asserted in Psalm 139:14, "I praise *You* because I am fearfully and wonderfully made." And from

the moment you were born you were meant to function at a high level of *Energy*. How do I know that? Because Scripture states that you and every other person have been created in the very image of God, and He is the essence of energy.

Unfortunately, as many people are growing up, negative things sometimes impact their lives adversely, many of those things absolutely outside of their control, which lead to a damaging of the image of God in them. This is why in Lesson One I made such a big point of directing you to carefully read Lesson Two and then to move immediately to Lesson Three if you are either obese or very weak. Why? Because if you are either obese or very weak you are totally lacking in energy and self-confidence and desperately need what I'm about to share with you. It will teach you how to take control of your life and destiny and how to create the future you were meant by God to enjoy. And believe me, this will energize you!

Obesity and Weakness

If you are obese or weak, 99 times out of 100 it's because you were never taught the fundamental principles of good nutrition and exercise or the importance of maintaining a positive mental attitude and having an unshakable spiritual "grounding" that gives purpose and direction to everything you do and are. Am I saying it's the fault of your parents or family of origin? No! Emphatically, no!

The truth is *most*, not all but most, people pass along to their children the same teachings and lifestyle they received regarding diet, exercise, intellectual pursuit, spiritual practice, and everything else that went into the development of their lives. If, for instance, they were taught that life is unfair and that they were just a victim of circumstance, that's all they could pass along to you.

Bottom line: some of you were never given sound information or any kind of grounding with regard to any facet of your life because your parents didn't have it either. As a result, they could not give you what they did not have. So you can't blame them! In fact, fixing blame on anyone just gives you an excuse to remain exactly the way you are. And that's a dumb thing to do if you are miserable. You need to toss blame out the window. *It's time to break the mold!* In fact, from this moment on you will not focus on the bad things that have happened to you or that you don't want in your life. From now on you will focus only upon the things you want in your life. Positive things such as:

- A beautifully sculpted, lithe, athletic body.

- A keen, clear mind that allows you to focus your intellect and emotions with laser-like precision to discover solutions to every challenge you face in life.

- A wonderful, enriching, and rewarding intimate relationship with the mate of your dreams.

- A job or career that is fulfilling and that you look forward to doing every day.

- An unbreakable spiritual foundation that brings meaning and purpose to every facet of your life as well as the confidence that you never again have to face anything alone because your Creator is right there with you.

Get the picture? Good. Let's start. To begin, you need to do a complete self-assessment. You need to be brutally honest with yourself about where you are and how you got here. Hold nothing back. This is not about blame. It's about identifying the truth and taking *responsibility*. Responsibility means to empower yourself to *respond with ability*. Granted, this takes guts, especially if you are obese. Albert Einstein said, "You cannot expect to expend the same amount of energy to get out of a problem as you did to get into it." But if you have the guts to do what I'm about to ask you, I guarantee there is a way out of whatever situation you find yourself stuck in.

So let me guide you. First, I want you to make a list of everything you don't want in your life. Clearly identify what those things are. Take out a pen and get a lined notepad and write at the top of the page: "The Things I Don't Want in My Life." Now, beneath this headline, list *everything* that comes to mind. For example:

- I don't want to be fat.

- I don't want to be weak.

- I don't want to be addicted to nicotine.

- I don't want back pain anymore.

- I don't want headaches.

- I don't want to live in clutter.

- I don't want to buy my clothes at Huge and Huger.

- I don't want to be turned down for dates.

- I don't want to be afraid to be seen in a swimsuit at the beach.

- I don't want to be the brunt of anyone's jokes.

- I don't want anyone to ever kick sand in my face again.

- I don't want anyone to say "You'd be good looking if . . ."

You get the idea. It's not hard, but it's *essential*. So put the book down and start writing now! Please.

Do it now. Don't let 5 more minutes pass without having done this exercise. It is literally the first step to a bright new future that you deserve and can have—but you need to do it *Now!*

Okay, after you've finished the list of things you don't want, you are ready to make a list of the things you do want. Write anything on this list that you sincerely want. While it doesn't have to all be fitness related, be specific about fitness-related goals that you want to accomplish. So get that notepad out again and on a new page write the following headline. "The Things I Want to Create in My Life Within the Next 12 Months." For example:

- I want to be able to do 100 straight Furey Push-ups in flawless form within 5 minutes.
- I want to weigh 180 pounds and have a 32-inch waist.
- I want to wear clothes that are designed for athletic people.
- I want to learn how to SCUBA dive and become certified.
- I want to learn to play the piano.
- I want to purchase a new home.
- I want to double my current income.
- I want to attract the perfect mate into my life.
- I want to be the kind of person whom friends admire and respect.
- I want to look in the mirror and not only love the image I see, but also the person *inside* the image.

Okay; got the idea? Great. Take a few minutes and write at least the top 10 priority goals you want to achieve over the next 12 months. Do it now.

Congratulations. Now that you have clearly identified your goals, you have taken a gigantic step toward creating the life you want. Later on, you will want to go back and add specific details and really flesh them out. By doing so, you will dis-cover that the more vivid and specific the details, the better the results. The master key, however, is to identify what it is you want and to put it down on paper so that it is transformed from the realm of thought to the realm of tangible substance that you can see, read, and touch.

Choose One Goal

The next action step is to select one goal from your list that you can focus on and accomplish within the next month. Make it a short-term goal that is within your reach. Don't have any? Then write one. How about painting your garage or spare bedroom? Or doing that landscaping job you've been planning. It can be anything that will provide you with a quick reinforcement to show you that once you focus on something, *you can do it*. Once you start doing this, your creative power will surge, and you will feel energized intellectually, emotionally, and physically. In fact, it will become habitual.

One way to give yourself the kind of reinforcement you need is to utilize a method I learned from Matt Furey, the author of the best-selling *Combat Conditioning* book. Take several 3" x 5" cards and write your goal on more than one card. Tape one to the bathroom mirror or some other conspicuous place where you will see it and carry another one with you. Take the card out at various times throughout the day and read it with deep conviction. If you can, read it out loud. Then on the day you have accomplished this goal, write the completion date on the card and celebrate. After celebrating, put it somewhere where you can refer to it often as a visual reinforcement. In fact, it's a great idea to start a collection of "Goal Achievement" cards and be able to look at them often. This will be the reinforcement you need to reinvent yourself and start living the life of your dreams. From now on you will succeed because you are no longer a victim but are the master of your own destiny.

THE POWER OF BEING POSITIVE

Now that you understand the importance of taking control of your mind, I want you to be especially aware of the words you speak. Consciously take note of every word you choose and ask yourself if the words are self-affirming or self-defeating. Likewise, ask yourself if your words empower or diminish others. From now on you will say nothing that does not empower yourself or others. This alone will help you to become a more positive, dynamic, and vibrant personality. When you become positive and affirming of yourself and others, it creates a powerful force of magnetic attraction. *People will be drawn to you.* In fact, *you* may end up being the most powerful and positive influence in the lives of some people, and thereby be a catalyst in helping them achieve greatness.

This is also why I encourage you to consciously make a decision to never say anything about yourself that you do not wish to be absolutely true. Never underestimate the power of your words to heal or to destroy, to create and bring positive circumstances into your life. In fact, good things can't help but happen when other people begin to regard you as a source of positive reinforcement and inspiration. They will literally seek you out to work on their behalf. This can create marvelous opportunities for you in every facet of your life, especially in business.

I have watched countless times where a positive "lightning bolt" of a personality has far surpassed many others who had twice the level of education and experience in any chosen field as the "lightning bolt." And why was the "lightning bolt" given the opportunity over someone significantly more "qualified"? Most often because the "lightning bolt" projects a positive energy that people want. It's that type of person who wins and gets things done, whom others who don't know any better refer to as "lucky."

But it's not luck. It is a positive energy that both attracts and projects and literally creates positive circumstances.

Let me give you a few examples from history. The Bible records how Joseph was elevated from being a prison inmate in Egypt to the position of number two man in the entire empire, second only to Pharaoh. Were there not others vastly more qualified both in terms of experience and education than a young Hebrew slave who spent the last ten years of his life in prison? Of course there were! But they didn't have that intangible, that "energy," that Pharaoh saw in Joseph (not to mention God's amazing favor and wisdom resting on him).

Or consider the life of Napoleon Bonaparte, who in his time had a level of personal magnetism that has seldom been matched in the history of the world. It was reported and widely known that on many occasions when Napoleon was considering a man to elevate to the rank of Field Marshall, he would listen intently as his staff told him of a potential candidate's experience and credentials. However, after listening for several minutes Napoleon would often interrupt them and ask one question upon which he would make his final decision. That question was: "Is he lucky?" And of course he wasn't talking about luck. He was asking in a roundabout way: "Does this man have the personal magnetism and charisma that creates positive outcomes? Does he have what I have?" Keep in mind that Napoleon did not lose his empire until he began dissipating his energy and over the course of time lost both his charisma and ability to lead and inspire others.

So what has all this to do with you, and why am I focusing so much attention on your intellect, emotions, and energy? Because in order for you to have abundance in all areas of life, in order to move up to a superior level of life, in order to have the good things of life, your mind (intellect and emotions), body (the part of you that is seen in the physical world), and spirit (the *you* in control of mind and body) must all be moving in the same direction. When that happens, what is commonly referred to as "miracles" begin to happen almost routinely. But can having this positive mind really create the positive circumstances I have been maintaining in this lesson? You better believe it can. Here's an example that showcases precisely what I have been sharing with you both in its most positive and life-affirming form and also in its most negative, life-destroying form.

In an article published in 1957 by psychologist Bruno Klopfer in *The Journal of Prospective Techniques*, a man called Mr. Wright suffered from advanced lymphatic cancer. His lymph nodes were swollen to the size of oranges, and both his spleen and liver were so enlarged that 2 quarts of milky fluid had to be drained from them daily. The doctors had done everything medically possible in the mid 1950s on Mr. Wright's behalf, but there was nothing more they could do. So they gave him up to die.

Somehow Mr. Wright heard of a new experimental drug for cancer. But it was only being administered to people whom doctors believed had at least a three-month life expectancy. Wright begged his doctor for the drug, and finally the doctor relented. According to the report, the doctor injected him on Friday but really didn't expect him to live through the weekend. Unbelievably, on the following Monday, less than 72 hours later, Wright was walking around and feeling great. The tumors had "melted like snowballs on a hot stove." Ten days after his first *Krebiozen* injection, Mr. Wright went home from the hospital being determined by the doctors to be *cancer free!*

Unfortunately, months later the American Medical Association published a nationwide study on *Krebiozen* that flatly announced it was worthless. Mr. Wright read the study, believed it, and his cancer returned. Two days later he died.

So what happened to Mr. Wright? Why did he become wrong? Let's examine it objectively. Mr. Wright, who is terminal, hears about a new miracle cure for cancer. He reasons to himself that the reason he has not already died is because it is his destiny to be cured of cancer and *Krebiozen* is the agent of that cure. He begs his doctor to go outside the rule and inject him. Then Mr. Wright's intellect and emotions, his mind, *believes* that the miraculous cure has been found, and as a result his body obeys the single congruent message that it is given by Mr. Wright's mind which is—HEAL! And his body has no other choice but to obey!

Just think what would have happened had Mr. Wright not read the study that negated his positive belief. Who knows how long he could have lived? But the simple point is this: Whatever you believe about yourself, both intellectually and emotionally, will determine who and what you become physically and spiritually. For that reason alone you must guard your thoughts, your speech, and all of your associations. If you surround yourself with positive reinforcement in what you see, hear, think, and verbalize, and if you follow through with positive action—you will meet with a positive outcome. It is inevitable!

Your Body

No matter what shape you are in, I believe this is some of the most important information in the entire book. It holds the key to master level achievement and self-mastery in all areas of your life. So let's apply this principle of being positive to your body and how to create the physical image you have always wanted.

If you are obese, it's time to give you a specific program that will clean your body from the inside out and then a program of exercise that will sculpt, strengthen, and reshape your body without putting your joints, tendons, ligaments, bones, and muscles in danger of injury. To accomplish this we will use Dynamic Visualized Resistance Exercises combined with the right aerobic exercises to totally transform your physique. But first you need to do a thorough internal cleanse.

"Man on extreme right is in desperate need of Kevin's magnifying glass." (see Intro of Lesson 4)
—J.P.

Internal Cleanse

When you look at this photo, ask yourself, *Do these people look like this merely because of soft abdominal muscles and a layer of fat?* Of course not. These people look like this because they have a great deal of body waste that is stored in their intestines and needs to pass. This condition can and does cause many serious and debilitating health conditions and is the first one that must be addressed if you are serious about sculpting your body and dramatically increasing your energy level. In fact, I have read autopsy reports about some of the most famous people in the world who died from health conditions directly related

to this cause. For example, when an autopsy was performed on Elvis Presley, it was determined that there was more than 40 pounds of impacted fecal material in his intestines. Think of it. Is it any wonder he looked so bloated at the time of his death? He was literally rotting on the inside. The amazing thing is that he managed to live to be 47 years old. It's very sad because had Elvis taken care of himself, had he eaten and exercised right and stayed away from drugs, he might still be with us today, and who knows how many hits he could have had and how much more enjoyment he could have brought to millions.

But now let's focus on you. Are you obese? Are you carrying around with you pounds of putrefying matter that needs to be removed from your body? If you are, the first step toward a remedy is the recognition of the *cause*. And for this reason I'm going to recommend that you go on a supervised internal cleansing program. The way to do this is to contact either a competent chiropractor, naturopathic doctor, or a medical doctor who practices complementary and alternative medicine. You'll be happy to know that you can have a complete list of more than 800 of America's leading complementary, alternative medical doctors by purchasing Dr. Valerie Saxion's best-selling book, *How to Feel Great All the Time*, which is available through Bronze Bow Publishing at www.bronzebowpublishing.com or toll-free at 1-866-724-8200. You can also contact Dr. Saxion directly at www.silvercreeklabs.com or by calling 1-817-236-8557.

An Exercise Program for the Weak and Obese

After you have achieved a thorough internal cleansing, it will be evident by how you feel that your body isn't nearly as far from achieving its natural perfection as you once thought. Now that you are armed with the right nutrition plan (Lesson Two), the ability to focus your mind, and having more energy than you can ever remember having, it's time to focus on the right exercise program that will sculpt and build lithe, shapely muscles all over your body while minimizing the potential for serious injury. It's time to create the body you've always wanted, and to do this we will utilize a method I call Dynamic Visualized Resistance Exercises or DVR. This is a method that was used by both Earle Liederman and Charles Atlas. Although I explained the method thoroughly in Lesson One, let's take a few minutes to review it.

As stated previously, many exercise systems can harm the body and hasten the aging process. Exercise machines and free weights can literally tear muscles, wear out joints, tendons, and ligaments, and damage the vascular system. Jogging, long distance running, and high intensity aerobics can injure bones in the feet, legs, and lower back as well as expend great energy needlessly. This type of overexertion eventually wears down the body, makes it susceptible to injury and disease, and can make you look far older than your years. This is why the late running guru, Dr. George Sheehan, wrote that "if you want to know what you will look like in 20 years, just look in the mirror after having run a marathon." Trust me. He was right!

The Wisdom of the Tiger. Tigers, lions, and even domesticated cats and dogs use an instinctual exercise system that helps them stay in peak condition throughout life and keeps them young right up to the time that death comes to claim them. This is what Charles Atlas based his exercise system upon and what I believe and teach. It is literally following the simple wisdom of tigers and other animals.

What is the system? Nothing more than stretching (extending and contracting) with great tension. If you watch a lion or tiger at the zoo or a household cat, this stretching takes only a few seconds and is done many times throughout the day as they move about and change posture. You'll notice that it stretches its entire body with great tension so much so that its limbs actually quiver. This is nothing like a man's yawning stretch or the way people have been taught to stretch to increase flexibility. Instead, this stretch is so powerful it actually builds muscles, and the tension is the secret. The inner resistance produced by the tension builds muscle fibers just as much as any form of external resistance whether by weights or machines. *But* since the resistance is perfectly controlled throughout the entire range of motion, no harm is done to muscles, joints, ligaments, tendons, or bones.

Translate these gentle yet powerful movements to an exercise system and you *energize* the body and fight the aging process by increasing blood flow through even the smallest capillaries, especially those located in the facial skin. One move in particular, the *high reach* seems to have curative powers (several of my friends have used it) to restore an injured shoulder to its normal range of mobility. And best of all, these exercises require no gym and no equipment. They can be done anywhere and at any time regardless of your size or shape and are the perfect complement to the strength calisthenics and dynamic self-resistance exercises I also teach. In fact, they are the *perfect* exercise system in and of themselves. On more than one occasion I have used them *exclusively* for weeks or even months at a time to rehabilitate from various injuries that have come from hang gliding and martial arts practice.

By the way, these techniques have been utilized for millenniums of time. Ancient martial arts masters spent a great deal of time observing animals to learn fighting techniques that they then incorporated in their martial arts systems. They also adopted tension exercises that they learned from animals. As a result some of these men developed extraordinary power that became a closely guarded secret right up to the twentieth century.

Getting the Best Results

To get the most benefit from this program keep the following information in mind:

■ **AEROBICS.** This DVR Exercise Program will develop your entire body. But I also recommend that you do a lot of walking each day. Try to walk at least 30 minutes each day at a good clip if you are keen on losing body fat. Swimming is also a great addition. I don't recommend running or jogging, however, until you are in really great shape because it can be very jarring to the body.

■ **FREQUENCY.** DVR exercises can and should be done each day. At first you will be using relatively light tension that will allow you to complete 10-12 repetitions per set before the muscles feel fatigued. At that point you will go immediately to the next exercise and progress through the entire series of 12 exercises, doing 10-12 repetitions each. Then you will repeat the entire circuit of 12 exercises at least once but preferably twice more for a total of 2-3 sets of 10-12 repetitions for each exercise.

Once you have mastered the movements you can apply greater tension. Your sets and repetitions will then change to reflect the following:

REPETITIONS		SETS
MODERATE	8-10	3 max
HEAVY	6-8	2-3 max
VERY HEAVY	3-5	2 max

■ **TENSION.** As stated in Lesson One, the key to the system is the amount of tension used. When you are starting out, vary the amount of *tension* until it feels comfortable. If you use only a small amount of *tension*, you will maintain muscle *tone* (I hate that word), but not build muscle. Too much tension can strain tendons and ligaments and even cause headaches. The right amount will develop the muscle fibers every bit as much as weights or machines but without the debilitating effects.

Several men have used these exercises to sculpt their bodies and build tremendous strength. Martial arts legend John McSweeney used this method exclusively to build his strength and maintain his physique and could throw an overhand right with the power of a young Rocky Marciano when he was in his 70s. So follow the guideline given above and realize that these exercises can be every bit as taxing as weightlifting. A word to the wise: Don't overdo it.

■ **BREATHING.** DVR exercises should be performed slowly and with great tension while breathing deeply. Breathe using both nose and mouth. Inhale on the way back (or up). Exhale on the way forward (or down). Between exercises practice power breathing from Lesson One. Remember the words of Farmer Burns: *"Deep breathing alone* has made many a sick man well, and many a weak man strong."

THE DVR ROUTINE

This routine consists of twelve exercises, and each one is vital in that it targets different muscle groups:

1. Neck Roll

Stand with your feet side by side, hands at your side, and slowly roll your head to the right while contracting the muscles in your neck. Circle all the way around for one repetition. Continue until you have completed 10 reps. Then reverse direction and complete 10 more while circling to the left. Start with light tension and gradually build.

2. Atlas Biceps Flex and Press

Stand with your feet at shoulder width apart and arms extended (horizontally). From photo #1 move through photos #2-3, powerfully contracting biceps. Extend arms (vertically) with great tension as shown in photos #4-5. Return back to starting position under great tension (photo #6). Continue until you have completed 10 reps.

3. High Reach

Stand with your feet at shoulder width and elbows bent, hands at shoulder height. Reach as high as possible while moving with great tension, one arm at a time. Use great tension in both directions. Palm can be open or hand can be clenched in tight fist to develop forearms.

4. One Arm Chin

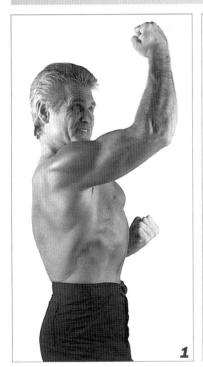  

Stand with feet at shoulder width and hands in fists. Lift one arm above your head (see photo) and pull down with great tension (imagine doing a pull-up with one arm) toward the center-line of your body. As one arm pulls down move the other to the up position. Once again use great tension while pulling to the center line. 10 reps for each arm.

"It is not because things are difficult that we do not dare, it is because we do not dare that they are difficult."

—SENECA

87

5. Full Range Pectoral Contraction

Stand with your left foot in front of your right foot and knee bent back straight (approximately one step, see photo). Hold hands in front, palms facing each other. Bring your hands back slowly with great tension until you feel your back muscles fully flexed. Hold for a count of one thousand one. Then move the hands slowly back to the original position while using great tension in your arms, shoulders, and pectoral muscles. Yes, the muscles will quiver.

6. Deltoid (Shoulder) Roll

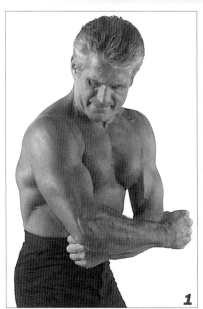  

Stand with feet at shoulder width, knees slightly bent, and back straight. Hands in fists and both arms bent (see photo #1), roll arms and shoulders back until your back muscles are flexed. Hold for one thousand one. Then roll forward until your arms cross one on top of the other, right over left, then left over right, switching with each rep until you have completed 10 total reps (5 right over left, 5 left over right). Keep forearms parallel to the ground and shoulders low. This is a superb movement for the deltoids, arms, and pecs.

7. Wrist Twist Triceps Contraction

Stand with feet side-by-side, arms straight in front and close to your body (see photo #1), with fists turned in (backs of hands almost touching). Rotate arms as in photo #2, turning fists slowly until they turn out. Flex the back muscles and contract the triceps as hard as possible for one thousand one. Then slowly reverse arms, returning to the start position with great tension. Arms remain down and fully tensed during entire movement. 10 reps.

8. Deltoid Raise

Feet side by side, hands in fists, feel tension in entire arm. Then slowly and with great tension raise your arms until they are extended overhead (photos #1-4). Reverse the movement, maintaining tension until your arms are at the starting position. *Don't just drop your arms!* Both movements should be done with great tension. 10 reps.

9. Biceps/Triceps Contraction

Standing with feet side by side, arms at sides, hands in tight fists facing forward (up), wrists flexed. Slowly and with great tension bend your elbows and curl your hands to your shoulders, contracting biceps as hard as possible. At top of movement reverse direction of your palms (palms point down, see photo #4) and slowly reverse direction and push down with great tension. At the bottom, flex your triceps hard. Reverse direction (palms up) and start the process once again. 10 reps.

10. Abdominal Contraction and Pull In (NOT PICTURED)

Stand with feet side by side, hands at sides. Press abdominal muscles down with great tension as you exhale. Flex muscles hard. Then pull in as hard as possible as you inhale forcefully. Create a strong vacuum. Hold for one thousand one. Continue for 10 reps, breathing with great force on both inhalation and exhalation.

11. Half Knee Bend

Stand with feet apart. Bend only halfway, but imagine you have a heavy weight across your shoulders. Feel extreme tension in the leg muscles as you slowly move down and up. Within a few weeks you will notice tremendous strength in your leg muscles and knee joints. 10 reps.

12. Calf Raise

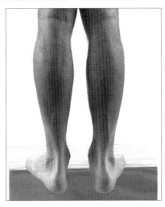 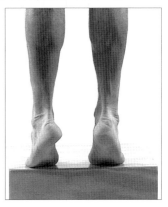

Stand with feet side by side. Have the balls of your feet either on a stair, a thick book, or even a piece of wood. Lower your heels and slowly raise up on your toes as high as possible with great tension. Lock your calves for just a moment at maximum tension, then slowly reverse direction and continue for 10 reps. Once you become adept at this exercise you can try doing it one leg at a time.

Muscle Size and Strength

Working out with DVR will require 20 to 25 minutes for a complete workout of 3 sets of 10 reps of each exercise. It can and will result in a dramatic increase in muscle size and strength as well as develop a sense of body awareness that allows you to contract any and every muscle group in your entire body at will. If after you are phenomenally strong you want to add other exercises, feel free to do so. You don't have to, but you certainly can, and thereby take your development to the epitome of strength and athletic development. Good luck, and please send me photos to let me see what you accomplish. In future editions of this book, I would like to have some of my best students model for the photos. I hope you will be one of them.

How to Become Spiritually Energized and Grounded

In order to become a fully self-actualized human being, you must discover the answers to the four universal questions that have always confronted the human race.

1. Who am I?

2. Where did I come from? (I'm not talking about your body. I'm talking about *you* inside your body.)

3. Why am I here? (What is my purpose?)

4. Where am I going?

Before I go any further, I will tell you that I have answered these four questions for myself. I found the answers to each question when I became a believer in and follower of the Lord Jesus Christ. And I encourage you to discover the answers to those four questions for yourself. In fact, there is no other way. No one can answer those questions for you. It's between you and God.

So how do you discover the answers? And how do you meet God? In my opinion, the best place to start is by reading God's Word, the Holy Bible. The Bible says that it is a self-revealing book, and I know that is true. It is literally God-breathed, and it will reveal its secrets to you if you read it sincerely with an open heart to receive the answers to your existence. The Bible repeatedly states that the throne room of the Lord of the universe is constantly open to you personally. You can contact God directly through prayer, speaking directly with Him, and there's never a waiting line!

As far as other insights and direction, I have none. It's not up to me or any other person to determine what is right for you spiritually or to tell you what is the right and only version you must believe or the denomination you must attend. Anyone who claims to have all the answers for you is on an ego trip, and you shouldn't give them the time of day. I know whereof I speak, because I grew up in an atmosphere where there were many self-appointed preachers who were more than willing to tell other people what to think, believe, and do. And in most cases the very people whom they were preaching at were already living more righteous lives than they were.

Bottom line: there are many people who would do themselves, God, and the people whom they preach at a big favor if they just *shut up*. Am I saying you shouldn't share your faith? Absolutely not. The fact is that every person you meet is told through your actions, including your words, who you are and what your faith is. And those actions speak louder than any words you could ever speak. For you, me, or anyone else to lay a religious trip on another person is to become nothing more than a pulpit-pounding prophet of religious paranoia. And no one needs that.

I have one personal account that illustrates my point. Back in 1990 I went through a painful divorce. As some of you know from experience, this is a terrible time to live through. And unless a person's heart is made of stone, he or she will go through a great deal of soul searching.

Shortly after my divorce was final, I had to attend a convention where many of my publishing clients were in attendance. At this convention there was a man who had recently become employed by one of my clients, and he had heard through the grapevine about my divorce. Prior to this employment he had been a competitor of mine in the field of graphic design and advertising and had not succeeded. Apparently he now felt that he could finally stick it to me by publicly humiliating me in his own sanctimonious way.

So in front of several people he started in on me about the rumors he had heard about my divorce and that I was a despicable sinner. I stood there and took it for two reasons. One, I wasn't about to do or say anything that would damage my business partner. And two, because as he vented his rage against me, I was acutely aware that he was doing this because he felt totally inadequate. The more he raged, the more I realized he was simply projecting a terrible self-loathing, and I was a vulnerable target to vent upon. Truly, it was a sad and pathetic demonstration of his own inner inadequacies. Even sadder was that he had the audacity to state that he was doing it for *my* own good, that he *loved* my soul, and *cared* about where I would spend eternity.

But did this man have any right to judge anyone? Not hardly. Although he had traveled around the country with his family to minister in churches through a musical ministry, did he live what he preached? No. This poor man lost everything he ever had when the IRS seized it for non-payment of income taxes. The only reason he evaded jail time was that he had not filed returns, and therefore he was not guilty of fraud.

I tell you this account to warn you about those who use God's Word as a weapon for their agenda rather than as an inspiration for your transformation. No one has the right to determine your spiritual destiny except you and God. Remember that. Keep it in perspective and realize that every life is tough and every person is continually on a journey of self-discovery. No one but God can give us the answers for our spiritual existence or purpose in life. All that God requires is that we live up to the light we have been given. If we live this way, when we leave this world it will be a better place for the fact that we were here.

I shall not pass this way again . . .

"I expect to pass through this world but once. Any good thing, therefore, that I can do or any kindness I can show to any fellow human being let me do it now. Let me not defer nor neglect it, for I shall not pass this way again."

—STEPHEN GRELLET, 1773-1855

Question & Answer

Q: Can I really get into great shape without going to a gym or hiring a personal trainer?

A: It is not necessary for anyone to go to a gym in order to perfect his or her body. As long as you have the will power and determination to succeed, you can accomplish even better results in the privacy of your own home, where the fullest concentration can be applied.

"The abdomen is the reason man does not easily mistake himself for a god."
—Friedrich Nietzsche

Crunch

LESSON FOUR

PUSHING YOURSELF
to **POWER**

ABDOMINALS

ABDOMINALS

"I have had dreams, and I have had nightmares. I overcame the nightmares because of my dreams."

—JONAS SALK, M.D.

Trim, rippling abdominal muscles are important to most people who work out. They are vital to the success of athletes in all sports and are essential to all combat athletes. The abdominal muscles protect the vital organs during physical contact and are responsible for the torso and hip movements. And strong, solid abs are probably the main reason the average fitness enthusiast hits the gym. Let's be honest, nothing looks better than a great set of abs.

Perhaps you've noticed that ab infomercials have all but replaced baseball as America's #1 pastime on both satellite and cable television. Whether it's the "Ab Shocker" or the "Carb Blocker," they all have this ridiculous feature in common—they promise beautifully sculpted abs that require no effort or self-discipline. Nothing could be further from the truth!

It's like what they used to say about isometrics back in the '60s: "Exercise effortlessly in just minutes a day." That was and is a crock. A true isometric is one of the hardest, most result-producing exercises you can possibly do. If you do an isometric correctly, the 10 seconds it takes are 10 of the most intense seconds you can spend. The same is true with abs. Pure and simple, it takes hard work—not lots of time, but hard, intense work—if you're going to achieve great results.

But as long as there are out-of-shape people looking for a "silver bullet," there are marketers from the P. T. Barnum school of marketing who are ready to profit with ab infomercials. Barnum's adage goes like this: "There is a sucker born every minute—and some to take 'em every 59 seconds." In fact, people who buy into ab infomercials have a lot in common with a friend of mine from high school.

Kevin was 5'6" tall and weighed nearly 300 pounds. Although he was terribly obese, he was the life of the party and kept me and all our friends laughing all the time—except in gym class. During the mandatory showers, he used to ask me if there was any way he could make a certain part of his anatomy more apparent. He even asked if Charles Atlas had any special exercises for it. I was honest with him and answered, "Kevin, you need to lose 150 pounds." But he loved his food, so that wasn't even negotiable.

Then one day Kevin came in all excited and showed me an ad in a men's magazine that promised, "Appear Larger Instantly! Guaranteed!!" He was so convinced this was his answer that he sent in a $19.95 money order. About four weeks later he came running to my school locker to show me that the package had arrived. Opening the box, Kevin pulled out a $.99 magnifying glass with instructions detailing how close to look at himself in order to "appear larger instantly!"

Whoever wrote that ad had an "off the wall," if not wicked, sense of humor. Yes, it's true you could say it worked. In fact, it probably worked better than 99 percent of the ab gismos on infomercials. That said, let's look at a real ab program that truly delivers great results—Guaranteed!

AB SCULPTING PROGRAM

The following ab sculpting program is second to none for developing beautifully shaped, strong abdominal muscles with deep separation. If you follow it closely along with the dietary recommendations of Lesson Two, it will take you as close as you can possibly get to looking like a living, breathing Greek sculpture. And trust me, you won't need a magnifying glass to see the sensational results.

As far as results go, a person who begins the program with an average amount of body fat will start seeing their abdominal muscles at about the time he or she can do sets of 10 repetitions on all 10 variations as presented here.

The program is comprised of 10 variations of "The Crunch." The Crunch is a perfect example of exactly what I have already made reference to several times throughout this book. It is an exercise that combines Dynamic Self-Resistance and Dynamic Visualized Resistance. It can be made supremely difficult and effective by adding an Isometric Contraction at the very top of the movement or at the moment of strongest contraction. In fact, once you learn to "crunch" properly, it will help you master all forms of DSR and DVR.

THE POSITION

The *ideal position* for your hands in the performance of the Crunch is shown in photo #1. Please pay special attention to it.

If you are incapable of performing the exercise as in photo #1 due to neck pain or weakness, then use the following method that I devised for my friend Dr. Byron Armstrong. This method requires the use of a large bath towel. Study the photo #2 carefully. You will position yourself so that the towel extends below your buttocks and above your head. Then you will grab the two corners of the top of the towel as pictured. Your head and neck will be comfortably cradled, and you are now ready to begin.

1

2

CR-1

Lie on a carpeted floor or mat and place your hands either as shown in photo #1 or photo #2 from the previous page. Your knees will be bend with your feet about a foot from your hips. The knees are together, and feet should be positioned with toes as shown. With your lower back tight to the floor and pushing down, begin to roll your shoulders up. When your peak contraction is achieved, hold it for a count of "one thousand one, one thousand two." Then slowly and under complete control return to the starting position. This is one complete repetition. Start with 5 repetitions and add a maximum of one rep each week until you reach 10 reps per set. There is no need to ever go beyond 10 if you do these with deep concentration and with an isometric peak contraction on the last rep. This is also true in the 9 variations that follow, in which only the foot and leg positions vary. These changes emphasize different areas of the abdominal muscles and ensure you a complete workout for every aspect of the abdominal musculature.

CR-2

In this variation the lower abdominal and oblique muscles on the sides of the waist are affected by opening the knees wide and pressing the bottom of your feet together. As before, raise and lower, holding to peak contraction for a count of "one thousand one, one thousand two."

CR-3

Raise your legs with your knees together and toes turned in to work the lower abdominal rows. Follow the same procedure as above, achieving peak contraction for a count of "one thousand one, one thousand two." Are you surprised by the intensity of 5 reps?

CR-4

This variation exercises the obliques and lower abs from a new angle. Legs raised, knees opened wide, and place the bottom of your feet together. Once again, raise and hold your peak contraction, then lower.

CR-5

The center of the midsection is worked when the legs are straight up in the air. As in previous sets, slowly raise, contract deeply, and lower.

CR-6

Lock the knees and spread the legs to work the upper abdominal row. Think about each repetition. Concentrate on the muscles being worked.

CR-7

This is a very difficult variation, but the results are worth it. The left leg is held straight, six inches off the ground, while the right leg is bent 90 degrees. Switch position of legs and repeat.

CR-8

The obliques are worked by bending your knees and raising and lowering the upper body in a controlled turn at the waist. A partner may be used to help keep your knees down. Perform an equal number of repetitions on both sides of body.

CR-9

From position shown in photo #1, simultaneously raise shoulders and knees as shown in photo #2 holding peak contraction for "one thousand one, one thousand two."

CR-10

From position shown in photo #1, curl pelvis forward and raise and pull knees as close as possible to forehead, as shown in photo #2.

One More Thought...

"THE SILVER BULLET"

Over the years I've been asked by many friends if there isn't a single ab exercise that does it all. Just one "silver bullet" that if practiced consistently would do the job. Well, truth to tell, there is! And it's the exercise you see me performing here. It's called "The Superman Wheel Push-up." This one exercise truly does it all.

But there is a problem with it. Guess whom you have to be in order to do it even once. Hint: "It's a bird . . . it's a plane . . ."

Question & Answer

Q: Why are you so down on professional bodybuilding?

A: Because real life is not mere pleasure or sensual gratification. Life is the performance of function, and the individual can live fully only when he performs every function—physical, mental, and spiritual—of which he is capable, without excess in any. If a man or woman becomes obsessed with the body only and the gratification of animal desires, he or she ceases to function as a complete person.

How often have you read about a bodybuilder or a pro athlete dying at a relatively young age because of all the chemical abuse he or she has put their body through. That's not living. That's not freedom. That's living in a self-created prison. And if the individual doesn't wake up and break free of the mindset that has entrapped him or her, he or she will die as a consequence.

Does that mean I am against physical self-mastery? Obviously not, or I wouldn't be writing and teaching others how to achieve it. What it comes down to is this. You do not want physical self-mastery for the simple gratification of animal desire. That is not life. Yet the performance of every physical function is a part of life, and no one lives completely who denies the impulses and needs of the body as a normal and healthful expression through self-mastery. Hence it is only logical that you would simultaneously develop your body, mind, and spirit to the pinnacle of their natural, God-given expression.

Tension

NECK

The Furey Bridge

LESSON FIVE

PUSHING YOURSELF
to POWER

All right you stiff necked infidels who think a nicely sculpted, lithe and supple neck isn't important. It most certainly is! And endorsed by no less an authority than King Solomon himself. If you think I'm kidding, just read the following quote:

"A man who remains stiff necked after many rebukes will be suddenly destroyed—without remedy."

—King Solomon
Proverbs 29:1

NOW, GET WITH THE
PROGRAM! PRONTO!

NECK

When I look back on it, I find it interesting that Earle E. Liederman and Charles Atlas offered what appeared to be contradictory advice as regards the muscular development of the neck. Liederman stated several times in his course that it was not possible to overdevelop either the neck or the biceps. Atlas, on the other hand, actually made statements about an ox developing huge muscle mass by tugging against a heavy load, whereas a lion has a beautiful symmetry and incredible athletic strength created by doing exercises of the type that he taught. When I read that section of Atlas's course, I was certain that Mr. Atlas was finally sticking it to the weightlifting establishment that had been constantly criticizing and badmouthing him and the methods he taught. In case you wonder, let it be known that I side with Charles Atlas.

This reminds me of an encounter I had 24 years ago. I was running around Lake Calhoun in Minneapolis after karate practice when a man came up to me, told me his name, and said that with my bone structure and his tutelage I could be "Mr. America." All I needed was 35 pounds of muscle mass in just the right places and I'd be set. I was 26 years old at the time, had a 48" chest and 28" waist (same as today), and the guy talking to me looked like a sideshow freak. I had no intention of giving up my 182-pound physique to look like some overdeveloped gorilla on steroids, and I politely declined his offer. I later found out that he was the preeminent steroid dealer in the entire Upper Midwest until he ended up doing several years in the penitentiary (bad choice of words—he was never penitent). This same freaky guy died several years ago as a direct result of all his steroid abuse.

I bring this incident up because this guy literally looked like the "ox" that Charles Atlas had referred to, though at the time I really thought he was much more of a male donkey (get it?). That said, let's look at the neck.

The first muscle group everyone sees when they meet you is the neck. So its development is an easy way to project an athletic "first impression." And although the neck is critically important in many sports, very few exercise programs deal with the muscles of the neck. For this reason I have included a series of exercises that develop the neck from all angles and directions. *Be very careful in your performance of these exercises. Take it easy at first and gradually build your strength. If you rush, you'll end up with a stiff, sore neck. Be warned!*

NE-1 (DSR)
NECK FORWARD CONTRACTION

Bend your neck as far back as it will go and place your hands across your forehead. Now slowly bring your head forward and resist the movement slightly with your hands. Vary this by bringing your head slightly to the right and then slightly to the left, resisting with your hands. Repeat several times. As your strength increases, make the resistance more powerful. Once the neck muscles are acclimated, you may include isometric stops at various points in the range of motion. However, when you do so, gradually increase the resistance and gradually release resistance after 10 seconds.

NE-2 (DSR)
NECK BACKWARD CONTRACTION

This exercise is the exact opposite of NE-1. The neck is bent forward with hands behind your head. Resist with your hands while endeavoring to force your head backward. When well conditioned, add isometric stops at any point you wish.

NE-3 (DSR)

Bend your head to the left as close to the shoulder as is possible. Now place the right hand on the right side of your head and force your head to the right, resisting powerfully with the right hand. Try to touch your right ear to your right shoulder. Continue this 3-5 times. Then reverse the movement, beginning with the right ear to the right shoulder and moving your head to the left against the resistance of your left hand. Once again, after the muscles have become stronger, you may add 10-second isometric stops at any point in the range of motion.

NE-4 (DSR)

Turn your face to the right. Place your hand on your forehead as pictured and resist while trying to turn your face to the left. Now turn your face to the left. Repeat 3-5 times. Now turn your face to the left and resist by placing your left hand on your forehead and endeavor to turn your face to the right against strong resistance. These are powerful exercises for the neck, and isometrics stops may be added.

NE-5 (DVR)

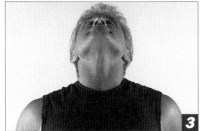

Anytime you do strength exercises for the neck, it is a good idea to end the session with neck rotation exercises to loosen and lubricate the neck joint. This is how it's done.

Bend your head far forward, chin on chest. Slowly bend around to the right, then backward and around to the left and around to the front. Make 3-5 complete rotations. Then reverse direction to the left. When doing this exercise, do it *slowly* and *vigorously* with tension. Don't do it as one guy I watched who went so fast he got dizzy and ended up falling down! That's a definite no.

NE-6 (DVR)

Throughout the day, the following exercise as well as NE-7 are excellent stress releasers. While standing, bend your head forward and carefully contract the front neck muscles as if trying to push your chin into your chest. Hold for a slow count of ten, then maintain your tension and slowly turn your face right as far as possible and then left. One complete rep is all that is necessary.

NE-7 (DVR)

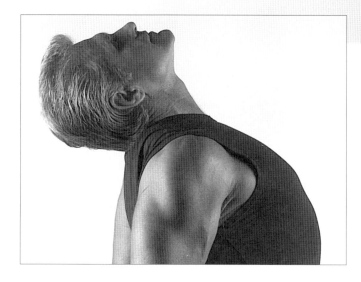

This is the same as NE-6 but in reverse. Bend your head far back and contract your neck muscles for a slow count of 10, then look right and left while maintaining the tension.

One More Thought...

If you are a grappler, a martial artist, a football player, or currently involved in any contact sport, the Furey Bridge is a superb exercise to add to your repertoire. It is actually a combination of power calisthenics and isometric contraction. However, it is not an isometric in the usual sense of the word because once you develop the ability to do it correctly, you then hold the position for 3 minutes or longer. I personally practice this exercise every day for a minimum of 3 minutes.

As with just about everything else in life, there is more than one way to do this. In fact, with this exercise there are two ways: the **wrong way** and the **Furey way**.

NE-8 (PC/ISO)
THE FUREY BRIDGE

Photo 1 shows the **wrong way**. Don't feel bad. That's how I did it until the fall of 2000. It's the way just about everyone does it.

Photo 2 shows the **Furey way**. I know it seems extreme, but once you work up to it, your flexibility will be nothing less than incredible and wall walking will seem like child's play—because, by comparison, it is!

Question & Answer

Q: John, in terms of raw strength and functional, all-around fitness, who would you say as a group are the best conditioned athletes?

A: Good question. I recently went to see the Cirque du Soliel, and there were athlete/performance artists, both men and women, doing physical acts that defy belief. But I doubt that that is the sort of thing you were referring to.

As far as amateur athletes are concerned, I doubt that anything requires more strength and all-around functional fitness than competitive rock climbing. These are some of the world's best athletes. When I've read about some of their training programs in climbing magazines, I've noticed that many of them who can do 3 or 4 consecutive full range pull-ups from a dead hang with 150 percent body weight. In other words, a 170-pound man can do 3 or 4 consecutive pull-ups with an additional 85 pounds of weight attached to his body, making him weigh 255 pounds. That is very impressive.

But the most impressive thing I've ever read was about one of these incredible athletes who did 3 consecutive pull-ups with 200 percent body weight. Using our 170-pound man as the example, that would be the same as doing 3 full range pull-ups with 340 pounds. To my way of thinking, that is nothing less than sensational.

Shoulder Roll

SHOULDERS

LESSON SIX

**PUSHING YOURSELF
to POWER**

*"Nothing is so strong as gentleness,
and nothing is so gentle as true strength."*
—Ralph Sockman

Deltoids

SHOULDERS

Once when I was a kid, I was watching a Western with my brother when my dad and three of my uncles walked in and decided to watch with us. These battle-hardened WWII vets were always up for a good Western. As it turned out, the big shootout between the hero and the bad guys started, and after shooting three of the "prairie scum" (as my dad so appropriately called them), the hero took a bullet right in the shoulder. Guess what happened? Nothing! The hero kept on going as though nothing had happened.

At that point my dad and my uncles all started laughing, and my uncle Milo said, "Johnny, I thought you boys were watching a Western, but I see we're actually watching Superman."

When I asked why they were all laughing, they told us that during the war one of the worst wounds you could get was to the shoulder. I didn't quite get it back then, but years later when I injured my shoulder (see the Matt Furey Profile), I knew exactly how incapacitating a bad shoulder injury can be. Which is why I'm paying special attention to the shoulder muscles here. I don't want you to experience the agony I did for 12 years until I met Matt Furey.

From the get go, I want you to take care of your shoulders and develop the muscles from all angles. Carefully following these exercises will go a long way toward keeping the entire muscle and joint structure of your shoulders strong and pain free for life.

That said, let's get to the 17 muscles in your shoulders. Their individual names are not important. What is important is that all of them are properly exercised. I am providing you with 14 exercises that can and will develop *all* of them.

SH-1 (DVR)
McSWEENEY HIGH REACH

This is the exact exercise that you will find in Lesson 3, number 3. I learned it from John McSweeney.

Stand with your feet shoulder-width apart and elbows bent, hands at shoulder height. One arm at a time, reach as high as possible while moving against great tension. Maintain maximum tension in both directions. Palm can be open or hand can be clenched in a tight fist to develop your forearms.

SH-2 (DVR)
SHOULDER ROLL

Stand with your feet at shoulder width, knees bent slightly, back straight, hands in fists, and one hand over the other as pictured (arms bent). From this position, roll your arms and shoulders back until your back muscles are fully flexed. Your arms should remain bent throughout the range of motion. Hold for "one thousand one," maintaining maximum tension. Then roll forward until your arms cross one on top of the other, right over left and then left over right, switching with each repetition until you have completed 10 repetitions (5 right over left, 5 left over right). Keep your forearms parallel to the ground and shoulders low. This is a superb movement for the deltoids, arms, and pecs. (see page 88)

SH-3 (DVR)
DELTOID RAISE

2

1

Stand with your feet side by side, arms at front, fists clenched, wrists flexed. Against maximum tension, *slowly* raise your arms outward and upward until they reach the position shown (do not fling them). At this point think into and powerfully contract your deltoid (shoulder) muscles. This is one of my favorite exercises. It is also great for stretching and limbering up. Do it often.

SH-4 (DSR)
FRONT DELTOID CONTRACTION

Allow your right arm to hang at your side and slightly backward. Now grasp the inside elbow (see photo) from the back by your left hand and endeavor to pull your right arm far forward, resisting powerfully with the left hand. This is a very short movement, only a few inches, but nonetheless a very powerful and result-producing exercise. Switch sides and continue.

SH-5 (DSR)

Bring your right elbow across the chest and grasp your elbow firmly with your left hand. Slowly force the right arm downward and backward against the powerful resistance supplied by your left hand. Repeat until fatigued, then switch arms and continue. This exercise strengthens the back of the shoulders.

SH-6 (DSR)

Grasp your right hand with the left hand in front (see photo). Gradually raise your entire arm outward and upward against the powerful resistance of your left hand. Repeat until fatigued, then switch arms and continue. Superb for outer shoulder muscles.

SH-7 (DSR)

Bend your right arm as pictured. Now grasp your right forearm from underneath and raise your arm outward and upward against the resistance of your left arm. This is a powerful movement for side deltoids.

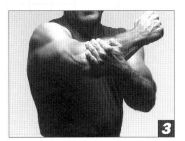

SH-8 (DSR)

With your arms straight, place your left hand over your right hand as pictured. Against the resistance of your left hand pulling down, raise your right arm until both arms are straight overhead. Reverse directions and lower against resistance. Switch to your right hand on top of the left and continue. With enough resistance, 3 to 5 reps is plenty.

SH-9 (DSR)

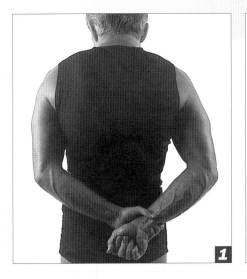

Place your right arm down against your side with your hand slightly behind the centerline of your body. Grasp your right wrist with your left hand in back of you. Raise your right shoulder as high and as slowly as possible while resistance is powerfully applied by your left hand pulling downward. Switch sides when fatigued and continue. Remember, you must use strength to build strength. This powerful exercise is for the trapezius at the top of the shoulder.

SH-10 (ISO)

While standing with your arms behind your back, grasp your right wrist with your left hand. Slowly endeavor to straighten your right hand out and down. Now, while building tension to the limit, breathe in deeply, and then at the peak of the contraction slowly exhale making an "ssss" sound, counting to 10. Gradually ease tension. Repeat, grasping your left wrist with your right hand.

Only one maximum tension isometric is necessary from both sides. But remember— slowly build the tension and hold at the maximum, then slowly release.

SH-11 (ISO)
SAMSON PRESS OUT

In the Bible, the Israelite judge Samson demonstrated this exercise's technique between two temple pillars (Judges 16:26-30). Too bad for the Philistines that it ended being isotonic instead of isometric.

In your case, you will do it in a doorway. Your hands should be flat against the sides of the doorjamb at shoulder height. Press out while breathing in and build to maximum tension. Once at maximum tension, breathe out slowly ("ssss" sound) while maintaining for 10 seconds. Relax your tension slowly. (If you hear a loud cracking sound at any point during this exercise, reduce the tension immediately unless the bad guys are closing in.)

SH-12 (ISO)
LATERAL RAISE

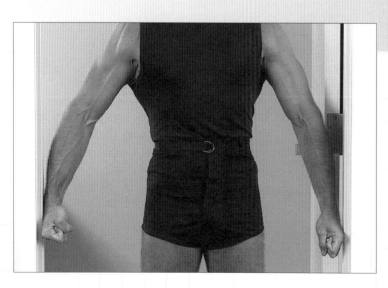

Do this one exactly as pictured. Build your tension to a maximum while breathing in. Hold your tension while slowly exhaling to a slow count of 10. Then slowly ease off the tension.

SH-13 (ISO)
POWER PUSH-OUT

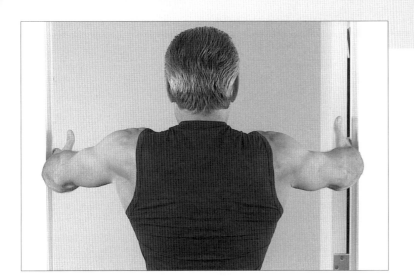

Position yourself as shown in the photo. Slowly build to maximum tension while breathing in. Hold your tension at the peak contraction while slowly breathing out.

Question & Answer

Q: John, I notice that you never use the word *"toning"* in your *Transformetrics*™ Program. Why is that?

A: You're right. I do *not teach, endorse,* or *use* the term *toning* because so-called toning exercises are for people who sit around watching infomercials for "Ab Shocker Electrode Devices" and other idiotic exercise gimmicks that promise "results with no effort." These poor people sit around the "tube" drinking beer and eating potato chips and actually believe it's possible to get something for nothing. *Toning* is the "catch" word used by virtually *all* the infomercials and magazine ads that sell devices, gimmicks, or exercise products that don't work. For that reason you will never read that word used in this book unless I'm defining it, pointing out something absurd, or having a little fun with an "off the wall" concept.

The *truth* is simply this: Either an exercise builds strength and muscle or it doesn't. Period. With *Transformetrics*™, you can dramatically increase muscle mass (size) or create traffic-stopping muscle definition (when you're on the beach). Either way, it's done by a combination of diet and high to ultra-high tension bodybuilding exercise that strengthens, shapes, and *builds* muscle. Any system that does not utilize building *tension* within the muscles simply doesn't work and is a waste of your time and money. Or as Uncle Wally would say, "You could do that until frogs grow feathers and nothin' is gonna happen."

One More Thought...

I want to encourage you that even if you do no other power calisthenics, do as many Furey Push-ups as possible every day. It is the single best exercise known for creating strength, flexibility, and endurance in the entire shoulder muscle structure.

BACK

LESSON SEVEN

PUSHING YOURSELF
to POWER

LATISSIMUS DORSI

*"Do not let what you cannot do
interfere with what you can do."*
—John Wooden

BACK

There's only one time I've ever heard of a man having a flawless "V" shape that worked against him. That was in Victor Hugo's *Les Miserables*. It seems Jean Val Jean had such an incredible "V" shape from spending close to 30 years as a galley slave that Javert could pick him out in a crowd. But then again, in the end, Javert does Val Jean a favor (you have to read it—I won't give it away), and the world ends up a better place.

While Val Jean is a notable exception, I can guarantee you many times to one that having a powerfully developed back will get you noticed in a very positive way 99.99 percent of the time. And the exercises that follow will help you achieve it on the hurry up.

In addition to these exercises, remember that all forms of pull-ups and push-ups from the Power Calisthenics Section are also awesome "V" builders. If you have any trouble doing them, however, stick with these for three months and pull-ups will no longer be a problem.

BA-1 (DSR)

Grasp both hands around your right thigh, as shown, just above the knee. Then with both arms pulling up, resist powerfully with the thigh. Perform 3 to 5 repetitions with extreme tension, then switch to your left thigh and do 3 to 5 more. This exercise is a powerful conditioner of both the upper and lower back muscles.

BA-2 (DSR)

While in a squat position (see photo), place your hands on the inside of your knees and then pull the knees apart while resisting powerfully with the legs pulling in. This movement is superb for the upper back, shoulders, and arms and also makes the muscles of the inner thigh more shapely. 3 to 5 ultra-tension repetitions are all that is required.

BA-3 (DVR/ISO)

While lying face down across a cushioned stool or chair, hands clasped behind your neck, simultaneously bend your head and feet upward. This is a very short movement. When your peak contraction is reached on your third to fifth repetition, try to hold for a 10-second isometric. At this point think into and powerfully contract your deltoid (shoulder) muscles. This is one of my favorite exercises. It is also great for stretching and limbering up. Do it often.

BA-4 (DVR)

Same position as BA-3 but with your hands now placed at lower back. First, bend the right side of your upper body upward (hold contraction for "one thousand one"), return to starting position, and then raise your body to the left. Repeat 3 to 5 times on each side. This will be difficult at first, but you'll be pleased with the results.

BA-5

Grasp your hands behind your back. Push your shoulders downward and backward and bend your head and back as far back as you can while powerfully tensing all of the muscles of both your back and neck. Hold peak contraction for a slow count of 10. 3 to 5 repetitions.

BA-6 (DVR)

Stand 18" to 24" from a wall with your arms fully extended above your head. Slowly bend backward under complete control, touch the wall, and then bend forward, coming as close as possible to touching the floor with your fingers. Perform slowly and feel your muscles contract and then stretch. An advanced version of this exercise is the Furey Wall Walk, (see BA-6B), but build up to this one *slowly*.

BA-6B (DVR)
FUREY WALL WALK

BA-7 (DVR)

With feet about 20" apart, bend down and touch the floor. As you come back up, fling your arms outward, upward, and backward as far as they will go. Repeat frequently throughout the day.

BA-8 (ISO)

With your hands directly in front of your chest, clasp your hands as shown—your right hand facing your chest (thumb and forefinger in up position), your left hand facing out (thumb and forefinger down). While breathing in, slowly build pressure as you pull outward to the maximum. At the peak contraction, slowly breathe out making an "ssss" sound. Hold the contraction for 10 seconds and slowly release. Breathe deeply. When recovered, reverse hand positions and repeat. Only 1 repetition of each hand position is required.

121

BA-9 (ISO)

While standing, lean forward and wrap your arms around your legs just above the knees, clasping your hands together. Attempt to lift your legs with your arms. Endeavor to lift from the shoulders and upper back to avoid placing undue stress on the lower back.

BA-10 (ISO)

With your arms straight above your head (as shown) and as far back as possible, grip your hands (left palm down, right palm up). Attempt to pull your hands apart. Follow standard isometric procedure. After completion, reverse grip and do one more repetition.

BA-11 (ISO)

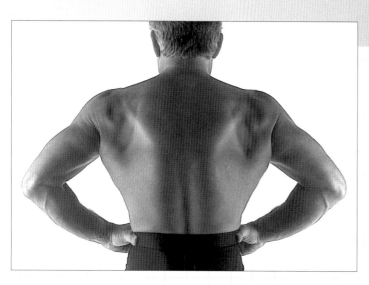

Place your palms against the abdomen, elbows out wide. Push against your abs while flexing the latissimus dorsi muscles (the two broad triangular muscles along the sides of your back). Flex as hard as possible for 10 seconds.

BA-12 (ISO)

 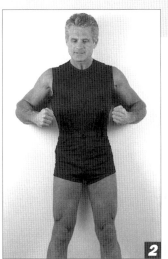 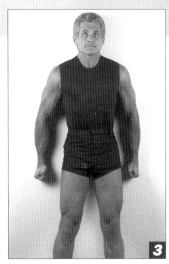

Stand with your back against a wall, arms bent as shown in photo #1 and at shoulder height with your hands at chest. Push your arms against the wall and hold peak contraction 10 seconds.

Photo #2—Repeat with arms in position shown.

Photo #3—Repeat 1 final repetition as shown.

BA-13 (ISO)

While seated, raise up on your toes as shown and place your hands around the fronts of your knees. With your fingers pointed inward and curling around your knees, pull straight back as forcefully as possible while simultaneously trying to lower your heels to the floor. Hold peak isometric contraction for 10 seconds. This one is great for the lats, abs, and forearms.

BA-14 (ISO)

Loop a towel over a door as shown. Pull out and down, build to peak contraction, and hold for 10 seconds. Gradually ease the tension.

One More Thought...

All fourteen of these special back exercises can and will develop the muscles of your back tremendously. In time, when used in conjunction with the arm and shoulder exercises, they will help you to do all variations of chins and pull-ups shown below. (Even if you can't do a single one at the present time.)

Regular Grip Pull-Up

Close Grip Pull-Up

Wide Grip Pull-Up

Close Grip Chin-Up

Cross Grip Chin-Up

Behind-the-neck Pull-Up

CONTRACT

BICEPS

"Keep away from people who try to belittle your ambitions. Small people always do that, but the really great make you feel that you, too, can become great."

—Mark Twain

LESSON EIGHT

PUSHING YOURSELF to POWER

Concentration Curl

BICEPS

"He trains my hands for war, so that my arms can bend a bow of bronze." From this scripture in 2 Samuel 22:35, it is easy to believe that King David was one powerfully developed man. If a man is so strong that he can actually bend a bronze bow as David did, and that man is an expert with the sling, is it hard to imagine that the velocity he could hurl a stone with would deliver a force comparable to shooting someone with a bullet? Think I'm overstating it? Then read the full account of his battle with Goliath in 1 Samuel 17. You'll see that I'm not, and though you may never need to bend a bronze bow or use a sling against a giant, wouldn't it be great to have a powerfully developed set of arms so you could defend yourself if the need ever arises? You bet it would.

With that in mind, you'll find that the exercises I present for both biceps (front upper arm) and triceps (back upper arm) are some of the best and most effective on this planet. Once you learn to do these exercises with focused intensity (DSR and DVR), only 3 to 5 repetitions are all that is necessary. And best of all, you can do all of the DSR and DVR exercises anywhere and anytime. I do many of these throughout my busy day. These exercises will also dramatically enhance your strength for all power calisthenics and sports.

BI-1 (DSR)
BICEPS CURL

Grasp your right wrist with your left hand. Your right hand is in a tight fist, palm up. You want to flex your wrist to engage the forearm muscles. Against the powerful resistance from your left arm, slowly curl your right fist to your right shoulder. Switch to your left side and continue.

REPETITIONS	
MODERATE	10
HEAVY	6-8
VERY HEAVY	3-5

BI-2 (DSR)
REVERSE BICEPS CURL

Same as above except that your fist is in a palm-down position.

REPETITIONS	
MODERATE	10
HEAVY	6-8
VERY HEAVY	3-5

BI-3 (DSR)
CURL FROM BEHIND

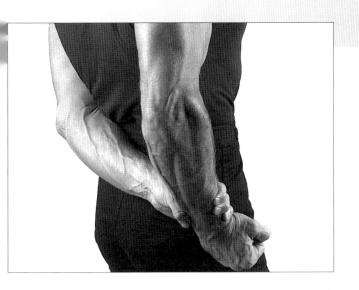

With your right arm down at your side and slightly to the rear, place your left hand in your right palm from behind and curl your right hand toward your right shoulder against the powerful resistance supplied by your left arm. This is a very powerful movement. Switch sides and continue.

REPETITIONS	
MODERATE	10
HEAVY	6-8
VERY HEAVY	3-5

BI-4 (DSR)

Grasp your hands in front, your right palm up and left palm down. Against powerful resistance, curl your right arm to your right shoulder. On the downward motion, resist strongly with your right hand, thus exercising the left triceps muscle. Study the photos and note that both arms have excellent leverage in this position. Switch arms and continue left palm up, right palm down.

REPETITIONS	
MODERATE	10
HEAVY	6-8
VERY HEAVY	3-5

BI-5 (DSR)

Same as BI-4 except your hands are clenched in fists, one over the other (see photo). Superb leverage allows you to apply maximum resistance from both arms. Switch arm position to right over left and continue.

REPETITIONS	
MODERATE	10
HEAVY	6-8
VERY HEAVY	3-5

BI-6 (DSR)

Same position as BI-4 only with palms down. Use powerful resistance. Switch arm positions and continue.

REPETITIONS	
MODERATE	10
HEAVY	6-8
VERY HEAVY	3-5

BI-7 (DSR)

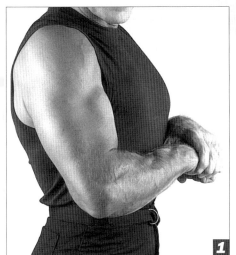

With your right upper arm at your side and your forearm across your chest, place your left hand over the back of your right wrist. Against powerful resistance, slowly raise your right forearm outward and upward. Your upper arm remains as close to your side as possible and does not rise at the shoulder. This is superb for the side muscle of the upper arm. Switch arms and continue.

BI-8 (DVR)

Clench your fists tightly and slowly curl both arms to your shoulder against visualized resistance, contracting your biceps as tightly as possible at the top of the movement. On the downward movement, turn the palms of your fist down and slowly extend. At the bottom of the movement, contract your triceps as strongly as possible. Continue on.

REPETITIONS	
MODERATE	10
HEAVY	6-8
VERY HEAVY	3-5

BI-9 (DVR)
CONCENTRATION CURL

While seated as pictured with your elbow on your right thigh, slowly curl your right fist to your right shoulder. Contract the biceps powerfully at the top of the movement. Continue and then switch arms.

REPETITIONS	
MODERATE	10
HEAVY	6-8
VERY HEAVY	3-5

BI-10 (DVR)
ATLAS BICEPS FLEX AND PRESS

Stand with your feet at shoulder-width apart and arms extended (horizontally). From photo #1 move through photos #2-3, powerfully contracting biceps. Extend arms (vertically) with great tension as shown in photos #4-5. Return back to starting position under great tension (photo #6). Continue until you have completed 10 reps.

BI-11 (DVR)
(NOT PICTURED)

With your right fist close to your right shoulder, practice powerfully contracting and then relaxing the biceps. This is a short but powerful movement. Repeat with your left arm.

One More Thought...

In addition to the biceps exercises found here, keep in mind that all forms of chin-ups and pull-ups work the biceps and forearms powerfully. If you currently have difficulty doing pull-ups, you won't after doing these exercises for a few months. *Guaranteed.*

TRICEPS

"Watch your thoughts; they become your words.
Watch your words; they become actions.
Watch your actions; they become habits.
Watch your habits; they become your character.
Watch your character; it becomes your destiny."

—Frank Outlaw

LESSON NINE

PUSHING YOURSELF to POWER

The C.A.T.

WRIST TWIST

TRICEPS

The triceps is the large muscle on the back side of your upper arm. When properly developed in conjunction with the biceps, it allows an athlete to accomplish some truly remarkable feats—such as hurling a stone at close to light speed (consider Goliath again in 1 Samuel 17), flattening an opponent with one punch after you've gotten your butt kicked for twelve rounds (reread the Rocky Marciano section), or even hitting a golf ball half again as far as some of your competitors (watch Tiger Woods). Not only that, but a well developed triceps has a very pleasing look to the eye as it assumes what is referred to as a horseshoe appearance on the back of the upper arm.

The triceps is a relatively easy muscle to develop. All forms of push-ups and dips develop the triceps. Not only that, but because of the way the human body is configured (or wired), it is not possible to develop the triceps without developing the shoulders and pectorals to some extent, and depending upon the exercise chosen, oftentimes to a great extent. In the power calisthenics section I give many more variations of push-ups and dips than either the Earle E. Liederman course or the Charles Atlas course. This allows you to attain far greater all-around development and protection from injury caused by overdeveloped muscles in one area while remaining undeveloped in another.

The exercises that are outlined here are superb for developing the triceps from a wide variation of angles and positions and are strictly of the Isometric Contraction, DSR, and DVR varieties. Even if you choose to never do push-ups or dips, these exercises alone could give you outstanding strength and beautifully shaped triceps.

TR-1 (DSR)
BLADE HAND PRESS OUT

With your right hand held as shown in the photo and with great power, slowly extend your right arm from just under your chin (elbows down) to a complete extension. Your left biceps is powerfully exercised during the resistance phase. A maximum of 3 to 5 reps is all that is required. Switch and repeat with your left hand. The superb leverage of this exercise makes it excellent.

REPETITIONS	
MODERATE	10
HEAVY	6-8
VERY HEAVY	3-5

TR-2 (DVR)
McSWEENEY WRIST TWIST

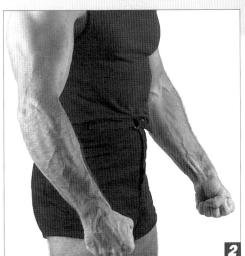

With arms in front as shown and backs of hands almost touching, slowly and with great tension rotate your arms back, turning the fists gradually until they turn out completely. At this point the triceps and upper back muscles are flexed powerfully, and you need to try to flex even harder for a count of "one thousand one," then slowly return to the starting position with great tension. If you exert extreme tension, 3 to 5 reps is all that is necessary.

TR-3 (DSR)
TRICEPS EXTENSION

Using the same grip as TR-1 except that your elbows are bent and both hands start behind your neck (see photo), press up and outward against extreme tension for 3 to 5 reps. Switch hands and repeat.

REPETITIONS	
MODERATE	10
HEAVY	6-8
VERY HEAVY	3-5

TR-4 (DVR)
THE C.A.T. (CHEST, ABS, TRICEPS)

Stand straight with your feet at shoulder-width apart. Start by bringing both hands (fists palm down) to shoulder level with your elbows lower. Push down with great tension. This is done by consciously contracting the biceps while extending down with your triceps. Extend down below waist level and slightly bend your knees. This exercise is superb for the pectorals, abs, biceps, and especially triceps. If you practice in front of a mirror, you will see that you are exercising your muscles in unison.

TR-5 (DSR)
BACK FIST DOWN

Hold your right fist palm up in your left hand. Slowly extend your right arm out and down against the strong resistance of your left hand pulling up and toward you. Switch and repeat, extending your left back fist and pulling with your right hand.

REPETITIONS	
MODERATE	10
HEAVY	6-8
VERY HEAVY	3-5

TR-6 (DVR)
CROSSING HANDS

Take a good look at the photos. This exercise is done at 3 levels, and each repetition the relative position of the hands changes—right over left, left over the right, 3 to 5 reps in each of the 3 positions. This is a powerful exercise for the abs, chest, biceps, and triceps, which receive an especially concentrated workout.

REPETITIONS	
MODERATE	10
HEAVY	6-8
VERY HEAVY	3-5

TR-7 (DSR)
TRICEP PUSH DOWN

Hold arms as shown (upper arms remain close to body throughout movement), left hand clasping back of right fist at centerline of body. While resisting powerfully with right arm, push down and out with left hand. After completing one set, reverse arms right over left. This is a very powerful exercise—don't neglect it.

REPETITIONS	
MODERATE	10
HEAVY	6-8
VERY HEAVY	3-5

TR-8 (DVR)
VERTICAL PALM PRESS

With your hands at chest level and palms forward (see photo #1), push out slowly with great tension until you reach full extension (see photo #3). Return to the starting position and continue. This can also be done from behind. Use slow, concentrated tension.

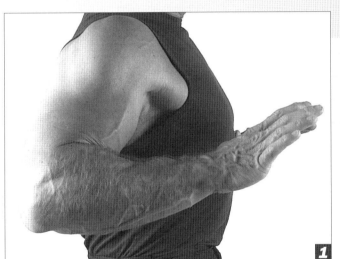

TR-9 (DSR)
FIST SALUTATION

While this may look much like the Liederman Chest Press, it is distinct (see photo #1). Notice that your right fist is in your open left palm. The range of motion is from the right to the left. Switch hand positions to your left fist in your right palm and continue. 3 to 5 full range reps is all that is necessary. And, yes, I know you feel it in your pecs, too.

REPETITIONS	
MODERATE	10
HEAVY	6-8
VERY HEAVY	3-5

Stand with your feet at shoulder-width apart and your left hand fingers touching your sternum. Extend your right arm to eye level. Clench fist as tight as possible and powerfully flex biceps and triceps with as much tension as possible. (photo #1) Now slowly extend your right hand down and across to your upper left thigh while the muscles of the entire right arm are powerfully contracted. (photos #2-3) (This and all DVR exercises will feel as though you are moving with the brakes on.) Return to eye level while maintaining maximum tension. Do 3 to 5 ultra high tension reps and then switch sides and do 3 to 5 ultra high tension reps with your left arm.

One More Thought...

PLEASE NOTE: All DSR exercises can be made into Isometric Contraction exercises by exerting so much force that no movement occurs. When this is done, remember to build tension while breathing in. Maintain maximum tension while breathing out slowly and making an "ssss" sound like air being let out of a tire and slowly ease off the tension. Don't hold your breath—you might blow a gasket!

Hammer Grip

FOREARMS

*"If 'just doing it' was all there was to it,
I would have already done it."*

—Mary Decker Tabb
Elite Runner

LESSON TEN

PUSHING YOURSELF
to POWER

WRIST

FOREARMS
WRIST, AND GRIP

Powerful forearms and a grip of steel not only look good but are absolutely essential in all combat type sports. But even in leisure, they can be very important.

Case in point. My wife and I were in Jamaica and took a catamaran cruise from Grand Lido Resort to Rick's Café in Negril, where you can dive from the cliffs or swing out on a giant rope swing and let go. I was having a great time on the swing and was in the water getting ready to swim back when I saw a man grab the giant rope to swing out. I had seen him on the catamaran and immediately knew he was so heavy that his grip couldn't support his body weight. So even though it was windy, I yelled at the top of my lungs, "Don't, Gary!" Unfortunately, he just barely heard me, waved in response, then grabbed the rope and tried to swing out. Instead he slid about 20 feet down the rope with his bare hands, then dropped into the water. When he surfaced, he was in agony with a capital "A." The friction burn had taken most of the skin off his palms and fingers.

I swam to him, did a cross-chest carry, and brought him back to the catamaran. My wife saw it happen, and without even thinking she dove in and arrived at the catamaran almost at the same time I did with Gary. To add insult to injury, everyone started asking the poor guy what happened. I looked at Denise and then said, "Gary, I yelled to you, 'Don't, Gary!' because you had suntan oil all over your hands." (He didn't, but I didn't want the humiliation to continue.) He caught on, and though almost in tears, he said, "I thought you said, 'Go, Gary!'" I got him to the nurses' station back at the resort and made sure that Dr. Jose Cuervo checked up on him and often.

End of story, with this moral. If you intend to go to Jamaica and use the rope swing at Rick's Café, spend three months prior to it doing the *Transformetrics™ Training System* with a special emphasis on this—Forearms, Wrist, and Grip. I guarantee you will be happy that you did.

The forearms are a muscle group that can sometimes be very difficult for certain types of physiques to develop. But pay special attention because these exercises are also the key to a world-class grip.

FO-1 (DSR)
WRIST CURL PALM UP

While seated as pictured, curl your wrist as shown. After completing with the right, reverse and continue with left.

REPETITIONS	
MODERATE	10
HEAVY	6-8
VERY HEAVY	3-5

FO-2 (DSR)
REVERSE WRIST CURL PALM DOWN

While seated as pictured with your palm down, curl your wrist as shown. After completing with the right, reverse and continue with left. Left hand supplies resistance.

REPETITIONS	
MODERATE	10
HEAVY	6-8
VERY HEAVY	3-5

FO-3 (DSR)
HAMMER GRIP DOWN

As pictured with left palm under right fist. Right hand curls down against resistance from your left hand. After completing with the right, reverse and continue with left.

REPETITIONS	
MODERATE	10
HEAVY	6-8
VERY HEAVY	3-5

FO-4 (DSR)
HAMMER GRIP UP

As pictured, left hand on top provides resistance to right hand curling up. After completing with the right, reverse and continue with left.

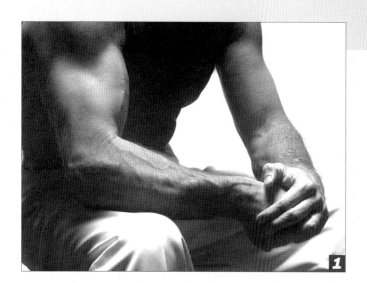

REPETITIONS	
MODERATE	10
HEAVY	6-8
VERY HEAVY	3-5

FO-5 (DVR)

Close your hands into tight fists. Extend your arms. Turn your fists inward and downward as far as they can be turned (see photo), then suddenly open your hands. Close hands, contracting powerfully, and again suddenly open. Continue until your muscles are fatigued.

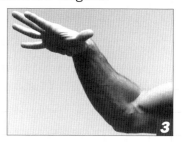

FO-6 (DVR)

Same as FO-5, only omit the opening sequence. Flex as powerfully as possible.

FO-7 (DVR)

With your fingers close together but open, bend the wrist in a full circular movement. First to the right, then to the left. This can be done with both hands at once.

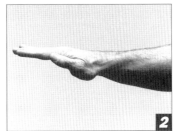

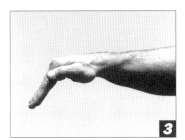

FO-8 (DVR)
(NOT PICTURED)

Get a large double sheet of newspaper and open it flat. With your arm outstretched, hold the sheet of newspaper with your fingers of one hand only. Starting at the corner of the sheet, roll up the paper to the size of a small ball in the palm of your hand. Repeat with the other hand. This is great for finger dexterity as well as forearms.

FO-9 (ISO)

Interlock the fingers of your left and right hands and as vigorously as possible try to pull apart.

FO-10 (ISO)

Grasp a broom handle or dowel as shown in these 3 possible grips for ten seconds and try as hard as possible to break it in half.

FO-11 (DSR/ISO)
(NOT PICTURED)

Squeeze a tennis ball, wadded up plastic bags, wash cloths, or a foam rubber grip for 10 seconds. Do it with each hand several times throughout the day.

One More Thought...

The above exercises will develop an awesome grip as well as power in the wrists, forearms, and fingers. Most can be done at any time throughout the day.

An additional exercise that can be done is what I call the Popeye Pull-up (see picture). This is a great exercise for the fingers, wrists, and forearms, but use FO-1–11 to build strength before doing this.

THIGHS

Lunges

LESSON ELEVEN

PUSHING YOURSELF to POWER

The Furey Squat

*"Nothing in the world can take the place of persistence.
Talent will not; nothing is more common than unsuccessful men with talent.
Genius will not; unrewarded genius is almost a proverb.
Education will not; the world is full of educated failures.
Persistence and determination alone are omnipotent."*

—Calvin Coolidge

THIGHS

As you might imagine, when a little kid spends the better part of four years on crutches, as I did from the lingering effects of polio, he often dreams of what it would be like to run and play like all his friends. As a result, by the time he discovers the leg development exercises as taught by Liederman and Atlas, he tears into them with a distinct passion. And guess what? They worked. Big time!

But I've got news for you. The exercises for leg development that I teach today are even better than those I learned over 40 years ago. Obviously, you've already been practicing two of them from Lesson One. I'm referring to the Furey Push-up and the Furey Squat. Both exercises are superior to the leg exercises I learned way back then. This is because the synergy of these two exercises creates a combination of exercise that develops the upper and lower leg muscles as well as the muscles of the hips from angles and directions that no other exercises can quite duplicate. So if you have not been practicing these two incredible exercises, or if you're slacking off on them, it's time to get your rear in gear and get moving.

The following exercises will not only strengthen and shape the muscles of your legs but will also develop what I refer to as "sustained strength" as is evidenced when you can do sets of 50 to 100 Furey Push-ups and can complete 500 or more Furey Squats in 20 minutes or less. When you can do that, you will have a level of both muscular and cardiovascular endurance that is off the charts by comparison to other methods of training.

Take a look at the leg exercises. I know that showing the Furey Push-up and Furey Squat may seem redundant, but they are key! So I'm showing them again (and besides, this is my book, so what are you complaining about?).

TH-1 (PC)
THE FUREY PUSH-UP

Photo #1. Start with your hands on the floor, shoulder-width apart, and your head tucked in and looking directly at your feet. Your feet are shoulder-width apart or slightly wider. Your legs and back are straight, and your butt is the highest point of the body.

Photos #2-3-4-5. Bend your elbows while descending in a smooth circular arc almost brushing your chest and upper body to the floor as you continue the circular range of motion until your arms are straight, back flexed, and hips almost, but not quite, touching the floor.

Photo #6. At the top of the movement, look at the ceiling while consciously flexing your triceps and exhaling.

Photo #7. Raise your hips and buttocks while simultaneously pushing back with straight arms, causing a complete articulation of both shoulder joints.

Photo #8. Arrive at the starting position with your legs and back straight, your head tucked in, and eyes looking at your feet.

Continue as smoothly and as fluidly as possible for as many repetitions as you can do.

At the beginning, anywhere from 15 to 25 repetitions is excellent. I know guys who can bench press 400 pounds who couldn't do 25 in a row if you had a gun to their head. Once you can routinely do sets of 50 or more, you will have superb shoulder, chest, arm, and both upper and lower back development.

In my opinion this is the single greatest exercise known to man because it exercises every muscle from your neck to your toes and on both front and back sides of the body. Repetition for repetition it delivers the highest level of strength, flexibility, and endurance of any calisthenic exercise known. In fact, it is the one exercise that comes closest to duplicating the exact movement of large jungle cats. It is truly one magnificent exercise.

TH-2 (PC)
THE FUREY SQUAT

This is definitely not your garden-variety knee bend. I consider it a close runner-up to the Furey Push-up in its order of calisthenic importance, only because it doesn't have quite the same overall bodybuilding effect. But it's close. When done in very high repetitions, I believe it is the world's preeminent cardiovascular exercise. Here is how it's done.

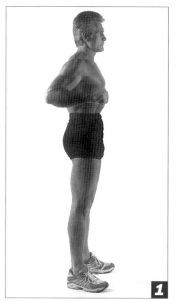

Photo #1. Feet approximately shoulder-width apart. Toes straight ahead. Hands in tight fists at shoulder level. Inhale deeply.

Photo #2. While keeping your back relatively straight (don't bend forward), bend your knees and descend to the bottom position.

Photo #3. Note the position of the hands reaching behind your back during the descent and brushing your knuckles on the ground at the bottom (how's that for a knuckle dragger?).

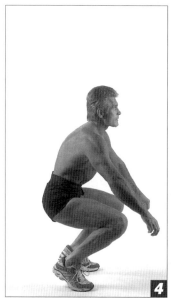

Photo #4. When you arrive at the bottom position, you will rise naturally to your toes. This is superb for your balance.

Photo #5. At this point your arms continue swinging forward and upward while simultaneously pushing off your toes and rising to the original standing position.

Photo #6. Your hands now form tight fists close to your sides at chest level. Inhale as you pull them in, exhale as you lower your body.

Repeat as smoothly and steadily as you can. Once you begin you'll notice that the arms take on a smooth, rhythmic motion similar to rowing a boat.

The entire movement of steps 1 to 6 is one continuous, smooth movement. 25 to 50 repetitions is a great start. 100 without stopping is excellent. Once you can do 500 in 20 minutes or less, you have accomplished the world's preeminent cardiovascular workout, not to mention a superb upper and lower leg workout.

FOR THE TRULY HARDCORE

For men and women who are already in phenomenal shape, try the one-legged squat which is shown to the left.

If you can do 10 with either leg, you're *a man*—even if you happen to be a woman, *you're a man.*

146

TH-3 (DSR)
LEG BICEPS CONTRACTION

Study the photos carefully. While standing on your left leg, slowly bend your right leg at the knee and raise your right heel as close as possible to your right buttocks. Contract powerfully for a count of "one thousand one, one thousand two." Then straighten out your leg until you are standing on both feet again. Continue 3 to 5 high tension repetitions and do an Isometric Contraction on the last repetition only. Switch legs and continue.

TH-4 (ISO)
WALL SQUAT AND HOLD (NOT PICTURED)

Stand with your feet approximately 20" from the wall. Slowly lower your body into a parallel squat. Your back should be touching the wall. Once you reach the parallel position you will hold as long as you can—up to 3 minutes. Yes, the muscles will shake. One repetition only.

TH-5 (DSR)
LEG EXTENSION

While standing on your left leg, raise your right leg to the position shown with your knee bent, toes pointed. Slowly, with great concentration, extend your right leg, endeavoring to fully extend and straighten it. 3 to 5 reps max. Switch legs and repeat.

TH-6 (PC)
LUNGES

Hands on hips. Take a step forward while bending the left knee and lowering yourself until your outstretched right knee barely touches the floor. Keep your left knee above your ankle as you bend very slowly, using your left quadriceps to control the motion up and down. Complete 3 to 5 high-tension repetitions (more if you want). Switch the relative position of the legs and repeat.

TH-7 (DSR)
LIEDERMAN LEG PRESS OUT

See the photos. This one looks odd and is not easy. Grasp your right heel with your right hand and raise your leg as high as you possibly can, extending against the resistance of your right hand until your knee is straight. It's the last part, the straightening of the knee that is most difficult. Do 3 to 5 intense reps with both legs (more if you want). This exercise develops the leg biceps.

TH-8 (PC)
SISSY SQUAT

I don't have a clue as to who named this exercise, but you don't have to be a pansy to do it! Have your feet about 12" apart and hands outstretched or on hips to keep your balance (see photo). Slowly lower your body by squatting down. Maintain the hips forward position throughout the exercise. Raise and lower slowly. 12 to 20 reps is great.

TH-9 (PC)
HIGH KICKS

Stand on one foot and practice kicking the other foot as high as you can. Practice kicking forward, backward, and to the side. This is great for the legs and helps develop your sense of balance.

TH-10 (PC)
THE ONE-LEGGED SQUAT

After warming up thoroughly with the standard Furey Squat, you may want to do one-legged squats and test the limits of your newfound strength and balance. Although this is a superb test of strength, it does not replace the Furey Squat where all 7 attributes of Dynamic Strength and Fitness are maximized.

One More Thought...

In addition to these incredible leg exercises, make it a practice to intentionally stretch and contract the muscles of the thighs and calves when out walking. Regular walking alone won't dramatically enhance your leg development, but consciously "thinking into" the stretching and contracting most certainly will. Practice this often.

Question & Answer

Q: By whose authority have you written this book? What organization has endorsed it?

A: What makes you think I need or want someone else's approval or endorsement? Is it not the very "earmark" of a slave to have to beg permission of his master to do something or be anything? I'm not part of that crowd. Never have been. Never will be. This book is about freedom from enslavement in all of its many forms. Its teachings are founded on truth. There is no higher authority than that.

CALVES

Balance

LESSON TWELVE

PUSHING YOURSELF to POWER

Calf Raises

*"To be always intending to make a new and better life
but never to find time to set about it is as...
to put off eating and drinking and sleeping
from one day to the next until you're dead."*

—Og Mandino

PUSHING YOURSELF *to* POWER

CALVES

et's be honest. Everybody has certain muscle groups that develop much faster than others. I'm of the opinion that genetics play a more than significant role in this part of the equation. Nonetheless, through diligence and perseverance even a kid rehabilitating from polio can develop a decent set of calves. However, it wasn't until I was about 13 years old that I'd allow myself to be seen in cut-off jeans, because until then my forearms were bigger than my calves. So even though I personally had to work my butt off to develop good-looking calves, I can tell you without a doubt that the exercises I'm about to show you can develop great calves if you have the genetics for it.

What do I mean by that? Well, it's like this. There was a stunningly beautiful dancer in one of my karate classes whom I started to date. After a late movie on a hot July night in 1977 we decided to go for a midnight swim in Cedar Lake underneath a beautiful moonlit sky. As we approached the water, I said, "My gosh, Linda, those are the most perfectly developed calves I've ever seen." She turned and replied, "You know you're the only guy in the whole world whom I know who would have noticed *that* under the circumstances."

So much for charm and romance. Sometimes you win; sometimes you lose. Sometimes you're the windshield; sometimes you're the bug. Sometimes you're the Louisville Slugger; sometimes you're the ball.

Bottom line: Young men, if your girlfriend has beautifully developed calves, she'd probably rather be complimented about something else.

That said, let's take a serious look at developing your calves. Because I've already given you such a wide variety of great exercises for the legs, and particularly the thighs, perhaps you're thinking this is too much. First, you need to realize that none of these exercises are all that difficult, and they can be practiced wherever you happen to be throughout the day. And, second, these exercises for the calves are truly important. A chain is no stronger than its weakest link, and one of the weakest links in many exercise programs and methods is that no emphasis is placed on developing balance alongside of strength and endurance. That's why these are so important. They will help you perfect your balance as well as strengthen the calf muscles.

CV-1

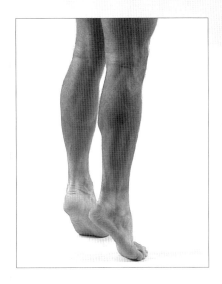

Stand with one foot a little in front of the other. Slowly rise as high as possible on your toes, trying to stand on the tip of the tip. (Hey, I said try. I'm not expecting you to be a ballerina.)

CV-2

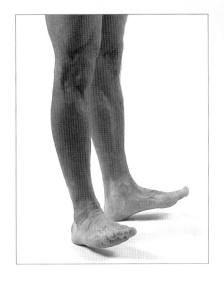

Stand with your feet 18" to 24" apart and support the weight of your body on the heels with the toes turned outward. Build the tension and hold for a "one thousand one, one thousand two." Then switch positions. Support your weight on your toes with your heels turned outward. Now slowly reverse it again. You'll notice that your feet come closer together with each repetition. Make sure you can consciously stretch and contract the muscles as much as possible.

CV-3

While standing on your right foot, raise your left foot from the floor and stretch it out as far as you can while pointing the toes downward. Switch legs and repeat. Contract the calf muscle powerfully, but go easy at first or you may get a charley horse.

CV-4

Same exercise as CV-3 except that your leg is stretched behind the body. Follow the same procedure and then switch legs.

CV-5

  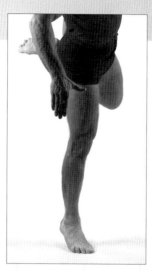

Rise up on your right foot as shown in the photos. You may hold on to the other foot. Slowly but powerfully contract the muscles. Yes, this is tougher than it looks.

CV-6

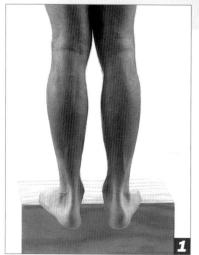 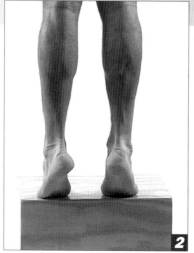

While standing with the ball of the foot on the edge of a chair, a step, or a thick telephone directory, rise on the toes as high as is convenient. Slowly and powerfully contract the calf muscles. Hold the peak contraction for "one thousand one, one thousand two."

CV-7

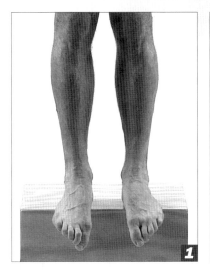
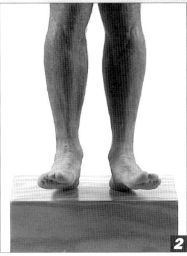

This time the heels are close to the edge, and the toes are lowered as much as possible. This looks easy, but looks are deceiving.

CV-8

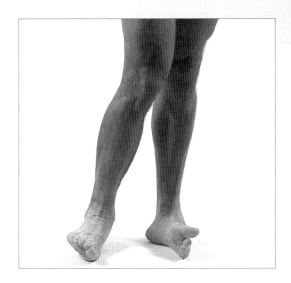

While standing on both feet, twist the left foot outward so that you are balanced on the blade of your foot. Your right foot is balanced on your right instep as shown in the photo. Lean your weight in the opposite direction to maintain your balance. Slowly switch to the opposite side. As always, consciously contract and stretch your muscles.

CV-9

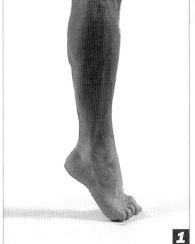
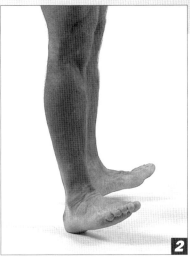

Stand on one foot and raise up on your toes as high as you can (see photo #1). Now rest on your heels and raise your toes (see photo #2). Switch feet and continue.

CV-10

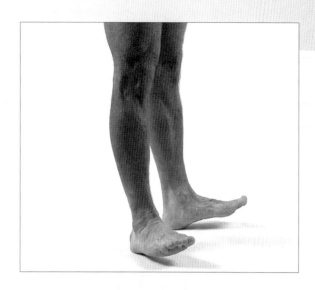

Stand on the your heels, toes up, bend the ankle and roll your feet outward until your weight is supported on the outsides of your feet. Then roll them inward so that your weight is supported on the insteps.

CV-11

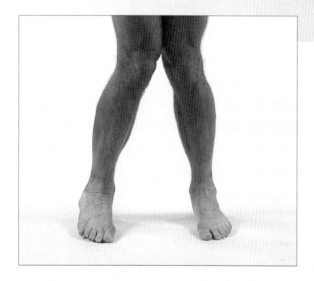

Similar to CV-10 except that you stand on your toes, rolling your feet until the weight of your body rests on the outside (blade) of your feet. Reverse and roll to the insteps. Try to do this without your heel touching the floor. It's a tough one.

One More Thought...

The performance of the calf exercises requires just a few minutes at any time during the day, but the payoff in improved strength and balance can be dramatic. And always remember that whether you're exercising your calves or any other muscle group that, just as it does in the dictionary, *effort* comes before *success*.

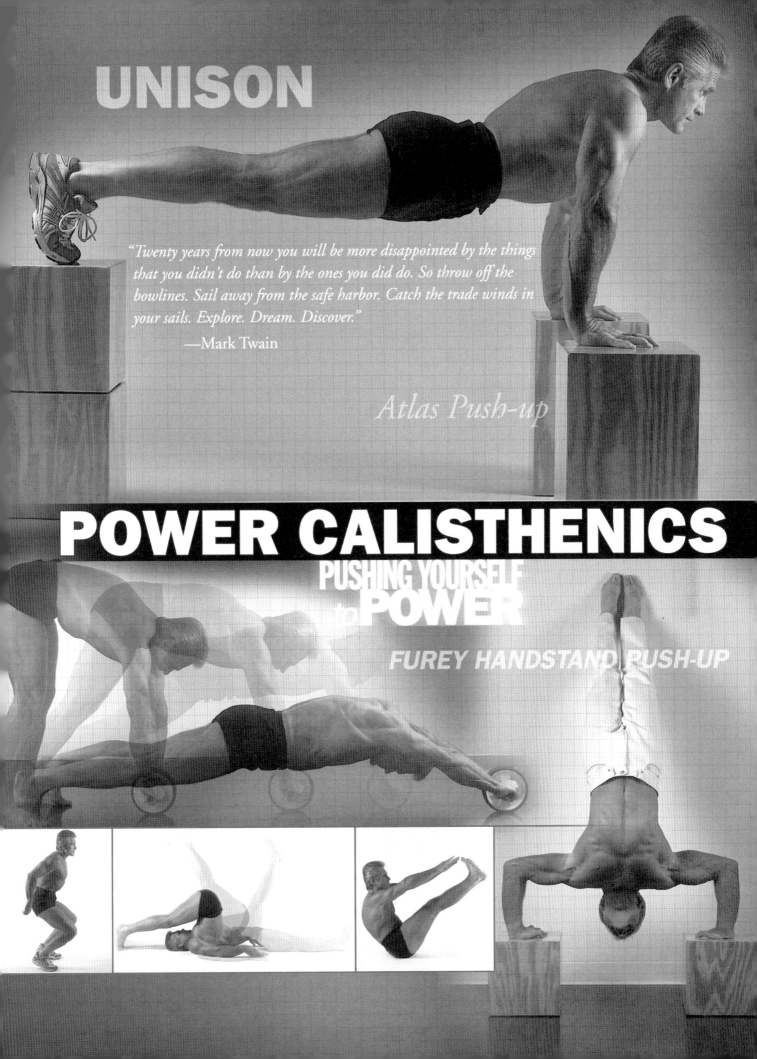

UNISON

"*Twenty years from now you will be more disappointed by the things that you didn't do than by the ones you did do. So throw off the bowlines. Sail away from the safe harbor. Catch the trade winds in your sails. Explore. Dream. Discover.*"
—Mark Twain

Atlas Push-up

POWER CALISTHENICS

PUSHING YOURSELF to POWER

FUREY HANDSTAND PUSH-UP

POWER CALISTENICS

In the 12 previous lessons I have taught you a series of exercises that will sculpt and strengthen every muscle from your neck to your toes. You have learned the basics of Good Nutrition in Lesson 2 as well as special motivational and self-empowerment techniques in Lesson 3 that will help you identify and overcome any obstacles to your continued success and happiness in any area of your life.

Now I want to focus on Power Calisthenics. You've already been introduced to the most essential ones: the Furey Push-up, the Furey Squat, the Atlas Push-up, and the Furey Bridge. These 4 exercises alone, if practiced diligently, will give you off-the-charts levels of all the 7 attributes of true dynamic athletic fitness and super health. The following exercises are other Power Calisthenics that you may wish to integrate into your program from time to time. They teach your muscles to work together in unison and can heighten the awareness you've already developed between your mind and your muscles.

Several times throughout the previous lessons I mentioned that besides those exercises there were specific Power Calisthenics that could also be used to enhance the other attributes of true athletic fitness. And I always told you that *even* if you can't do the calisthenics now (not a single repetition), you most certainly would be able to practice them in the future if you diligently practice the Dynamic Self-Resistance (DSR) and Dynamic Visualized Resistance (DVR) exercises. I can say that with certainty because the DSR and DVR exercises teach you how to think into and control your muscles. Once you accomplish that, the rest is simple.

I'm going to show you the Power Calisthenics in photos, but I'm not going to give detailed instructions on the performance of each. How they are performed is obvious from the photos. But I must emphasize that regardless of the exercise, do each one flawlessly with complete focused control. There should be no jerkiness at any point. Think into the muscles as you work them and throw arbitrary numbers of repetitions out the window.

Numbers: What They Mean and Don't Mean (a Fallacy Exposed)

There are many fitness experts who will tell you that if you can do X number of such and such an exercise, or if you can run X distance in Y time, you are in the beginner, intermediate, or advanced categories of strength and fitness. *From My Perspective This Is Wrong!* Let me give you some examples of why I believe that numbers in and of themselves are irrelevant and meaningless.

Every person, male or female, inherits a certain somatotype (body type) that is unique to himself or herself. Two people of the same height can have vastly different body types. This includes the length of torso in comparison to length of legs; width of shoulders in comparison to hips; length of upper arm compared to lower arm; length of upper leg compared to lower leg, and so on. Additionally, we are all born with certain ratios of fast twitch to slow twitch muscle fibers, which when taken into consideration with the previously listed factors determine whether we are made more for speed, or endurance, or a combination of the two. With the exception of genetically identical twins, no two people are exactly alike. And it is the combination of *all* of the above factors that determine your leverage, strength, and ability at certain sports, lifts, or exercises.

Take, for instance, my friend Dr. Scot Cressman. Doc is a huge, powerful man at 6'6" and 325 pounds. He is a member of the world famous Power Team, an evangelistic group that brings the gospel to youth and families worldwide. Doc can easily bench press over 400 pounds, despite the fact that he literally has to push it over a foot farther than other power lifters who are only 5'5" and have short arms. Yet even with his extremely long arms and tremendous muscle mass, he can still do 7 full range pull-ups (all the way up and all the way down), which is truly impressive. Still many so-called "experts" classify those 7 reps as only being in the "beginners" category. That's ridiculous, given all the factors concerning Doc's body type. And if you saw the feats of strength and power he routinely does, you'd see that he is in the top 1 percent of the world's strongest men.

Here's another example. I have another friend by the name of Troy Johnson, who is also 6'6" but only weighs 185 pounds. He has a lithe basketball body that is a muscular version of the actor Pierce Brosnan. In other words, his body looks as though it was sculpted in a wind tunnel, and all that's left is muscle and bone. At 82" from fingertip to fingertip, he's got extremely long arms and wide shoulders, yet Troy can do 12 pull-ups. Once again, to say that a guy this strong is only an "intermediate" is ludicrous. I'm not normally a betting man, but I would challenge the so-called "experts" to keep up one-on-one with Troy on a basketball court for an hour and then go to the pull-up bar and see

who can do more pull-ups. My money would be on Troy, and I think I'd make a killing.

Do you get my point? Don't get hung up on numbers. In and of themselves they mean very little. Don't get discouraged because you have a hard time with push-ups, pull-ups, or any other exercise because you may have poor leverage for doing them. In fact, be encouraged by this rather interesting "fact." The *poorer* the leverage you have for any given exercise, the more benefit you will get from performing it for far fewer repetitions than someone who does it with perfect leverage.

So don't go throwing in the towel because certain exercises are tough. After all, if it was easy, what would be the point in doing it? And by the way, it was for all the above reasons that neither Leiderman nor Atlas gave arbitrary numbers of sets and repetitions to be performed in their world famous courses. It's the same reason Matt Furey doesn't, and it's the same reason I don't.

Bottom line: you and your body are unique. No one else on this planet could possibly know how to train it as well as you will once you have the knowledge and experience.

That said, let's go to the Power Calisthenics and give you the knowledge so that you can gain the experience.

Success is the result of good judgment.
Good judgment is the result of experience.
Experience is often the result of bad judgment.

Bottom line: You're here to learn. And as long as you're learning, you can't be perfect or there would be nothing to learn.

GROUP I: NECK
1. FUREY BRIDGE

GROUP I:
2. REVERSE FUREY BRIDGE

Both of these Furey bridge exercises are for those involved in contact sports. Work up to their performance very gradually and if you feel any pain— STOP! They are both very advanced exercises and require the utmost of care and caution when performing either one.

GROUP II:
SHOULDERS, CHEST, TRICEPS, UPPER BACK, & ABS
1. FUREY PUSH-UP

See page 60 for complete instructions.

GROUP II:
2. STANDARD LIEDERMAN PUSH-UP

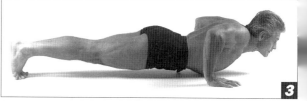

GROUP II:
3. LIEDERMAN PUSH-UP (VARIATION)

GROUP II:
4. STANDARD ATLAS PUSH-UP

GROUP II:
5. ATLAS PUSH-UP (VARIATION)

GROUP II:
6. TIGER BEND PUSH-UP

Start on forearms as shown in photo #1, apply pressure "straight down" on palms. Raising yourself to full extension as shown in photo #4. (yes, this time your butt is "up" in order to place more stress on the triceps.

GROUP II:
7. TRICEP PUSH-UP

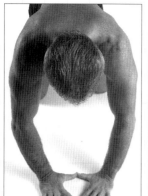

correct hand placement

GROUP II:
8. SUPERMAN PUSH-UP

Please Note: This exercise is very intense on the abdominal muscles as well.

GROUP II:
9. HANDSTAND PUSH-UP

GROUP II:
10. EXTENDED RANGE HANDSTAND PUSH-UP

GROUP II:
11. FREESTANDING HANDSTAND PUSH-UP

GROUP III: BACK, BICEPS, & FOREARMS
1. STANDARD PULL-UP

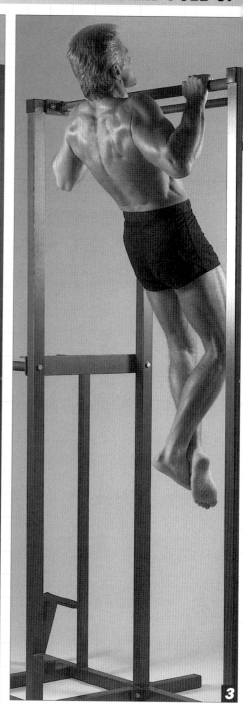

Please Note:
1. **ALL PULL-UPS** are performed with palms facing away from the body.
2. **ALL CHIN-UPS** are performed with palms facing the body.

This represents the distinction between a pull-up and a chin-up.

GROUP III:
2. WIDE GRIP PULL-UP

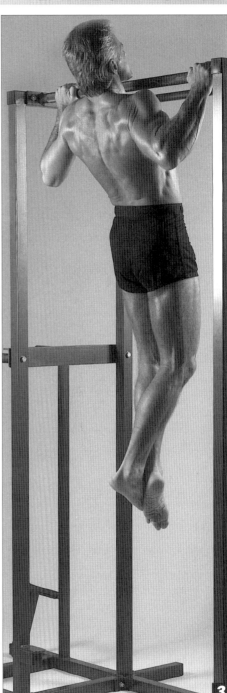

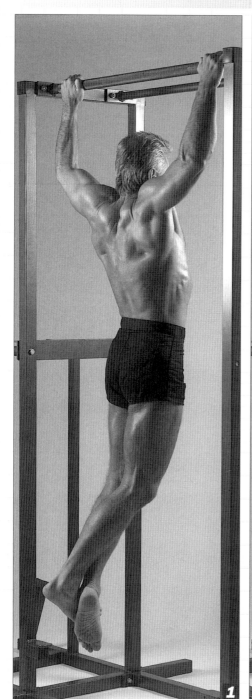

GROUP III:
4. CLOSE GRIP PULL-UP

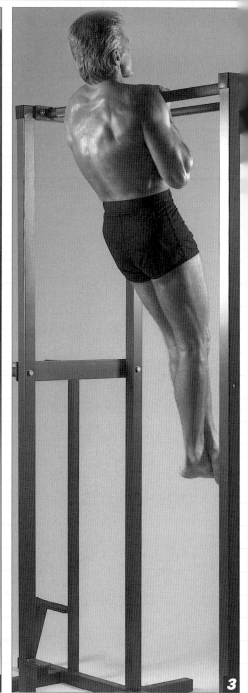

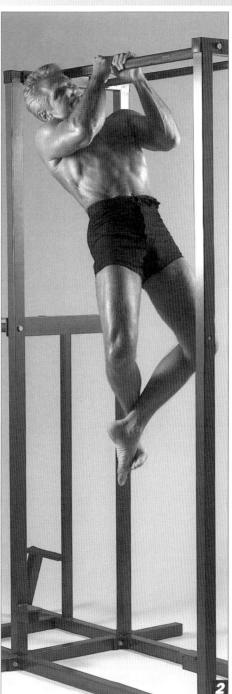

GROUP IV: ABDOMINALS
1. ATLAS SIT-UP

Anybody that says sit-ups don't work your abs has obviously never done Atlas sit-ups. Done full-range, forehead or chin touch your knees on each repetition. The secret is that the feet are *not* held down. It is muscle contraction alone that keeps them down. That is why this exercise works incredibly well. However, both this and the Atlas Leg Raise (Group IV #2) should only be done to your present range of motion. **So be careful.**

GROUP IV:
2. ATLAS LEG RAISE

(Full range dynamic flexibility)

GROUP IV:
3. ATLAS COMBINATION

(Strength, coordination, balance)

GROUP IV:
4. V-UPS

(Strength, coordination, balance)

GROUP IV:
5. SUPERMAN – WHEEL

If you can do five of these from a standing position, you're a man! *(even if you're a woman, you're a man!)*

GROUP V: UPPER LEGS
1. FUREY SQUAT

See page 61 for complete instructions.

GROUP V:
2. LEG EXTENSION

GROUP V:
3. LUNGE

GROUP V:
4. SISSY SQUAT

GROUP V:
5. HIGH KICK (FRONT, BACK, SIDE)

GROUP V:
6. ONE-LEGGED SQUAT

GROUP VI: CALVES
1. TOE RAISES

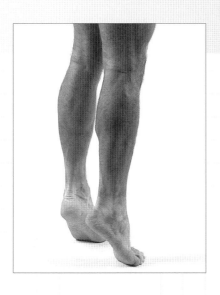

GROUP VI:
2. HEEL RAISES

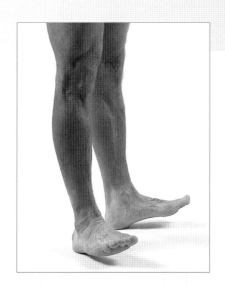

GROUP VI:
3. TOE EXTENSION

GROUP VI:
4. SINGLE LEG TOE RAISE

GROUP VI:
5. TOE RAISE OFF BOX

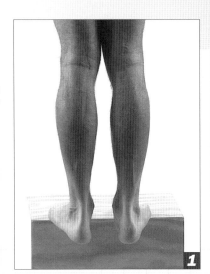 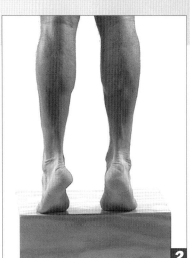

GROUP VI:
6. HEEL RAISE OFF BOX

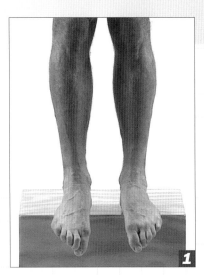 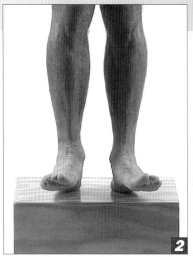

FROM 0 TO 500 PUSH-UPS IN 6 WEEKS OR LESS—GUARANTEED!

Earlier I mentioned that as a very young man I was doing 500 Atlas Push-ups each day in sets of 100. And though the results I achieved from it were fantastic in terms of my physique, the program I'm about to share with you will help you achieve even better results while protecting you from potential injury.

But before I get to the program, I want to review a few key points. The push-up in all its multiple variations has been a major part of the strength and physique development program of several world-class athletes—Charles Atlas, Earle Liederman, Woody Strode, Herschel Walker, and, of course, Matt Furey. You may want to take a few minutes to review the Hero Profiles at the beginning of the book. There are also many other famous actors and athletes who also emphasized the push-up as their personal cornerstone of strength and development. These include G. Gordon Liddy of Watergate infamy, Karl Gotch (known as "the God of Pro Wrestling in Japan" and teacher of Matt Furey), Master Jhoon Rhee of martial arts fame (who at the age of 72 continues to do 1,000 push-ups a day), Tony Curtis, Robert Conrad, Charles Bronson, and many others.

So you see, the concept of doing high volume push-ups every day is not unique to my program. In fact, in the June 2001 issue of *Iron Man* magazine, author Bill Starr wrote an incredible article in which he cited two examples of off-the-charts results that he had personally witnessed from men who used the push-up alone. The first was his friend Jack King of Winston-Salem, North Carolina, who was recovering from a near-death experience and found he could no longer do any upper body weight training exercises. By that he meant *none*. No flat benches, inclines, declines—*nothing*. So Mr.

Starr said that his friend improvised and did a partial push-up with his feet on a bench and his hands on blocks to take the pain and pressure off his wrists. Slowly but steadily Mr. King worked up to four sets of 150 repetitions. His payoff was rather astounding. Mr. King went on to win several physique contests, including the Masters Mr. America.

The other example Bill Starr cited was from his Air Force days when he was stationed in Iceland. A young corporal whom Starr knew had allowed himself to get into terrible shape and gained fifty pounds (all of it "ugly weight"). According to the article, this young man was eligible for a furlough soon and decided he wanted to look his best for his young bride, since he'd only been married a week before shipping off to Iceland. So this guy got his act together and stopped drinking booze and cut way back on his eating. Then he recalled how effective push-ups had been in boot camp, and he decided to go on a push-up blitzing routine.

But there was a problem. He was in such bad shape that all he could manage was a shaky 15 reps. Nonetheless, with a steely resolve this guy slowly but surely added both repetitions and sets. Starr said that every time he saw the corporal on base, whether in the rec room, the mess hall, or the barracks, he'd drop down and do a set of push-ups. He got to the point where he was cranking out 75 reps per set and completing 20 sets each day for a total of 1,500 reps. Starr said he had never seen anyone transform his body so rapidly and radically as this guy did. After less than one month he had an incredible physique with arms, chest, and shoulders that were truly amazing. As Starr said, "He looked as though he'd been doing advanced level bodybuilding for some time."

Okay, that's where Starr and I diverge. It never ceases to amaze me that people can be so programmed by the propaganda of so-called "exercise physiology" that they can't recognize the truth for what it is. And that is simply this. When you know what you're doing, *anyone* can achieve phenomenal results with body weight-only exercises. What Starr didn't recognize was that this young guy *was* on an advanced bodybuilding program, and the results spoke for themselves in less than one month. It makes me feel like saying, "Duh," when I read statements such as this. In fact, Liederman and Atlas and Furey would tell you that it's great but not surprising.

So now that I've made my point about the effectiveness of push-ups, let me show you a push-up blitzing routine that can help you add unreal size and strength in a short span of time. This program is far superior to my fanatical Atlas Push-up blitzing routine of over 30 years ago. As good as that was, I discovered later that it actually *caused* a problem. One that I didn't realize or correct until Matt Furey took me under his wing. Matt's philos-

ophy, and now mine, is to exercise every muscle group from as many angles and directions as possible. This ensures *complete* development, and minimizes *over*development in one part of a muscle group and *under*development in another. I'm convinced this is why I sustained such a terrible shoulder injury. My muscles were strong in one direction only, and weak in another. This is what Matt Furey helped me correct. That's also why I'm presenting the multiple variations in this program.

As far as number of reps per set is concerned, all that matters is that you start where you are and gradually add reps to each set as you are able. Keep in mind that you are *not* in competition with anyone. So please don't compare yourself to anyone. Six weeks from now you'll be able to do 500 push-ups each day, and it doesn't matter whether it's 5 sets of 100 or 100 sets of 5. Either way you will achieve incredible results, *especially* if you continue to do the *Transformetrics*™ DVR and DSR exercises. Now study the photos below. I want you to do as many variations as possible every day. This will enhance your all-around strength and fitness.

The Furey Push-up

Standard Liederman Push-up

Liederman Push-up (Variation)

Tiger Bend Push-up

Standard Atlas Push-up

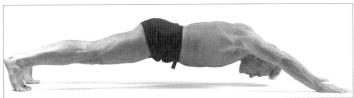

Superman Push-up

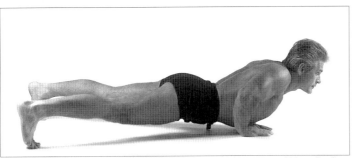

Tricep Push-up

Atlas Push-up (Variation)

Handstand Push-up

Extended Range Handstand Push-up

Freestanding Handstand Push-up

YOUR PERSONAL GUARANTEE

Now that you've read the book, I want you to ask yourself, What did I learn from this?

If your honest answer is nothing, then make an appointment with a competent psychologist and take this book with you to your appointment. Once there, hand it to them and have them smack you with it as hard as he or she can. Maybe that will knock some sense into you. There's no excuse for not learning everything necessary to transform your life and create the body you've always wanted. The principles in this book come from tried and proven methods used and taught by some of the world's greatest teachers, both past and present. None of what I teach comes from a think tank or some guy claiming he's discovered secret information buried in some lost monastery or secret Soviet archive. Everything I teach is the real deal!

GUARANTEED!

Now get to it. I'm pulling for you all the way.

Your Friend,

John E. Peterson

P.S. You can contact me through Bronze Bow Publishing at **www.bronzebowpublishing.com**. I'd like to hear from you and don't forget to send me your before and after photos.

NOTES

Unleash Your Greatness

AT BRONZE BOW PUBLISHING WE ARE COMMITTED

to helping you achieve your **ultimate potential**

in functional athletic strength, fitness, natural

muscular development, and all-around superb

health and youthfulness.

Our books, videos, newsletters, Web sites, and training seminars will bring you the very latest in scientifically validated information that has been carefully extracted and compiled from leading scientific, medical, health, nutritional, and fitness journals worldwide.

Our goal is to empower you! To arm you with the best possible knowledge in all facets of strength and personal development so that you can make the right choices that are appropriate for *you*.

Now, as always, **the difference between greatness and mediocrity** begins with a choice. It is said that knowledge is power. But that statement is a half truth. Knowledge is power only when it has been tested, proven, and applied to your life. At that point knowledge becomes wisdom, and in wisdom there truly is *power.* The power to help you choose wisely.

So join us as we bring you the finest in health-building information and natural strength-training strategies to help you reach your ultimate potential.

*W*HEREVER SHE GOES, VALERIE SAXION constantly hears this complaint: "I can't remember when I last felt good. I'm exhausted and rundown. How can I start to feel good again?" This book is Saxion's response to that question, but it goes far beyond just feeling good. "So why don't you feel *great* all the time?" she asks. "Why are you willing to settle for less than 100 percent?" She then lays out a *Lifelong Plan for Unlimited Energy and Radiant Good Health* to help readers give their bodies the opportunity to start feeling great in four basic steps.

Specifically, Saxion guides her readers into an understanding of how their bodies work, how to stop eating junk food, and the importance of body oxygen, exercise, and water. *Candida*, detoxification, fasting, low thyroid, and weight loss are all covered as well as establishing a perfect diet that is filled with foods that supercharge the mind and body. Nature's prescriptions of vitamins, minerals, and herbs supplement all that she teaches.

Includes a state-by-state list of more than 800 of America's leading complementary alternative medical doctors.

DO YOU HAVE A CHRONIC HEALTH PROBLEM that you just can't shake off? Perhaps you have intestinal problems that come and go? Recurring bouts with diarrhea? Or you're tired all the time and feel depressed? Have you consulted with your doctor but not found an answer? It is very possible that the cause of what you are experiencing is directly due to parasites.

Don't cling to the notion that parasites are limited to the Third World. Parasitic experts estimate that there are between 100 and 130 common parasites being hosted in the American populace today, and a recent health report stated that 85 percent of Americans are infected with parasites. The trick is that the symptoms caused by parasites are subtle because they are experienced commonly by people without parasites, and the vast majority of health-care professionals have little training in diagnosing these masters of disguise and concealment.

If you're alive, you're at risk of this hidden crisis that is damaging millions of people needlessly today. It is a lot easier to become a parasitic host than you think!

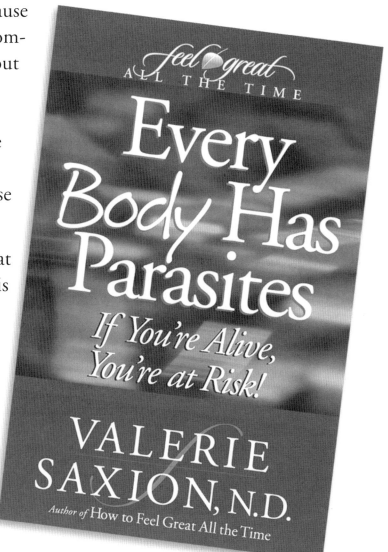

feel great
ALL THE TIME

Every Body Has Parasites

If You're Alive, You're at Risk!

VALERIE SAXION, N.D.

Author of How to Feel Great All the Time

THE EASY WAY TO REGAIN & MAINTAIN YOUR PERFECT WEIGHT

If you are among the 60 percent of adults in the United States who are classified as overweight and tired of trying one diet after another, now is the time to take control. The agonizing cycle of up-and-down dieting and seesawing weight can come to an end. There is a way to shed the extra pounds and maintain your perfect weight as well as restore your body to fullness of health. Dr. Valerie Saxion will provide you with a down-to-earth guide to weight management, nutrition, exercise, and health.

HOW TO DETOXIFY & RENEW YOUR BODY FROM WITHIN

If you are tired and rundown all the time, frequently irritable or depressed, or have chronic health problems, this booklet will teach you one of the most basic steps you can take to give your body the opportunity to start feeling great again. Cleansing your body of impurities and renewing it from within is simple, and it is wonder-working. It is totally doable, and you can start right where you are today. Dr. Valerie Saxion will direct you through a powerful purification plan that will help rejuvenate your body and unlock the secrets to an abundance of health.

CONQUERING THE FATIGUE, DEPRESSION, & WEIGHT GAIN CAUSED BY LOW THYROID

Millions of people are currently suffering from low thyroid and don't even know it. The symptoms can range from significant fatigue to depression to muscle swelling to low sex drive to an intolerance to cold temperatures. Yet many physicians do not recognize the phenomenal importance of the thyroid hormone to the overall health of their patients, especially among middle age women. Dr. Valerie Saxion will provide you with a practical program to help you determine if you have hypothyroidism, what its causes are, and how to deal with it.

HOW TO STOP CANDIDA & OTHER YEAST CONDITIONS IN THEIR TRACKS

If you have searched in vain for answers to health problems such as PMS, headaches, chronic fatigue, skin rashes, or poor digestion, it may be due to an overgrowth of *Candida albicans* or other yeast conditions. This parasitic yeastlike fungus will disguise itself in everything from athlete's foot to low blood sugar to obesity. It is estimated that over 90 percent of the U.S. population has some degree of *Candida* overgrowth in their bodies. Dr. Valerie Saxion will help you identify, treat, and overcome this hidden problem.

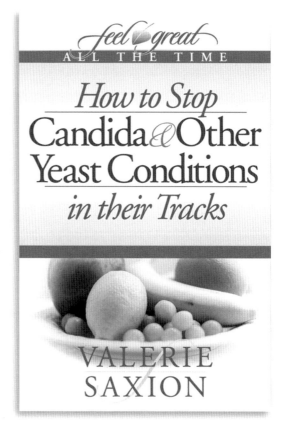

Navy SEAL Breakthrough to Master Level Fitness

Are you searching for the one exercise system that contains the exact same training strategies and technologies used to transform ordinary men into the world's most elite fighting force, the U.S. Navy SEALs? Look no further!

As a Navy SEAL, Mark De Lisle mastered the SEAL exercises and workout regimens and turned them into a powerful fitness program to help everyone, male or female, reach the pinnacle of athletic achievement and potential. His program has proven to build muscle, reduce fat, improve health, boost energy levels, and help individuals break through and reach their fitness goals.

Not all calisthenic programs are equal. Many target just one muscle group or are not laid out properly to give you maximum benefit. With Master Level Fitness, you'll systematically work each muscle group to its peak while performing a full range of motion exercises. By focusing on the entire muscle core and utilizing your own body weight, the program help you achieve optimal fitness and body transformation.

If you'd like to feel strong, confident, genuinely attractive, the real deal walking the streets with evident power and natural grace, the *Navy SEAL Breakthrough to Master Level Fitness*™ will make you the best you can be!

12 Weeks to Better Than Ever

Mark De Lisle's daily workout guide to his *Navy SEAL Breakthrough to Master Level Fitness*™. Everything you need to know to reshape, reenergize, revitalize, and renew every muscle in your body from head to toe in 12 weeks or less.